Para Maira
mi amiga
del borreg—Peña

THE NEW WORLD BORDER

GUILLERMO GÓMEZ-PEÑA

PROPHECIES, POEMS & LOQUERAS FOR THE END OF THE CENTURY

CITY LIGHTS
SAN FRANCISCO

10 9 8 7 6 5 4 3 2 1

Cover photograph by Martin Vargas
Cover design by Rex Ray
Book design by Elaine Katzenberger
Typography by Harvest Graphics
All photos and illustrations © the individual artists
English translation of "The Artist as Criminal" © 1994 New York University
and the Massachusetts Institute of Technology, reprinted with permission from
The Drama Review

Library of Congress Cataloging-in-Publication Data

Gómez-Peña, Guillermo.
     The new world border : prophecies, poems, and loqueras for the end of the
century / Guillermo Gómez-Peña.
          p.   cm.
     ISBN 0-87286-313-1
     1. National characteristics, American — Literary collections.
     2. Multiculturalism — United States — Literary collections.
     3. Millennialism — Literary collections.   I. Title.
     PS3557.0459N49   1996
     818'.5409 — dc20   96-1886
                                                                             CIP

City Lights Books are available to bookstores through our primary distributor:
Subterranean Company, P.O. Box 160, 265 S. 5th St., Monroe, OR 97456.
541-847-5274. Toll-free orders 800-274-7826. FAX 541-847-6018. Our books
are also available through library jobbers and regional distributors. For personal
orders and catalogs, please write to City Lights Books, 261 Columbus Avenue,
San Francisco, CA 94133.

CITY LIGHTS BOOKS are edited by Lawrence Ferlinghetti and Nancy J. Peters
and published at the City Lights Bookstore, 261 Columbus Avenue, San Francisco,
CA 94133.

ACKNOWLEDGMENTS

Since I never "finish" a text, there have been several versions (not just drafts) of most of the pieces included in this book, and there will probably be others which are yet to be realized. My performance texts and chronicles have included different collaborators at different times, and not all of them are represented in the versions which appear here, although I've tried to mention as many as I can. Anyone interested in other representations of my work can use the following list as a preliminary guide:

Freefalling Toward A Borderless Future was originally part of "Califas," a performance poem published in my first book *Warrior for Gringostroika*, Graywolf Press, 1993. Other versions have appeared in *Yale Theater Magazine*, Spring 1995, and "Border-X Frontera," a radio art piece anthologized in the double-CD collection of my audio work *Borderless Radio*, produced by Word of Mouth Music (Toronto), 1994.

Different versions of the **Free Trade Art Agreement** have appeared in *The Subversive Imagination*, edited by Carol Becker, Routledge Press, 1994, *Mapping the Terrain*, edited by Suzanne Lacey, Bay Press, 1994, *Grantmakers in the Arts Newsletter*, Spring 1995, and *High Performance Magazine,* Fall 1993.

Different versions of **The New World Border** have appeared in *Third Text*, Winter 1992, *High Performance Magazine*, Summer/Fall 1992, *The Drama Review*, No. 38:1, Spring 1994, and *Zurda* (Mexico City), 1994.

Real Life Border Thriller was first published in the *LA Weekly*, May 28-June 3, 1993.

The '90s Culture of Xenophobia appeared in the *Movement Research Journal,* Spring 1995, and an excerpt with the title "Beyond the Tortilla Curtain" was published by the *Utne Reader*, September/October 1995.

Chicanost: Radio Nuevo Orden was originally broadcast in 1991. A live performance version is included in the film *Naftaztec TV*, which was produced at iEar Studios at Rensselaer Polytechnic Institute in 1994. Another version can be found in the audio art piece "Ménage à Trade," New American Radio, 1994.

The version of **El Naftazteca: Cyber-TV for A.D. 2000** which appears here is an excerpt of "Naftaztec TV," a live TV broadcast produced at iEar Studios (see above), and first aired November 22, 1994 on Deep Dish Television.

The sections of **Borderama** titled "La Nostalgia" and the "Free Trade Art Piñata Party" appear in *Fronterilandia*, a film by Rubén Ortiz and Jesse Lerner. Also, various parts of the script have been performed live for Pacifica radio. Commissioned by the Washington Performing Arts Society and Gala Hispanic Theater, the first complete version of this project premiered in June 1995 in Washington, D.C. and was titled, "The Dangerous Border Game." Collaborators in different cities have included: Adalberto Arcos, Paulina Sahagun, Carmel Kooros, Norma Medina, Silvana Straw, B. Stanley, Michele Parkerson, Quique Aviles, Maria Elena Gaitan, Eugenia Vargas, Nao Bustamante, Sara Shelton Mann, René Yañez, Daryl Bates, Darren Chase, Christopher Dehm, Jennifer Gwirtz, Margaret Keenan Leonard, and Eric Pukprayura.

I have performed different versions of **A Seminar on Museum Race Relations** in collaboration with performance artist James Luna [at the Smithsonian Museum of Natural History and the Mexican Fine Arts Center Museum of Chicago] and with Roberto Sifuentes [occasionally as part of "Borderama"]. A printed version appeared in *Plazm Magazine*, Winter 1996.

Terreno Peligroso was originally published in Spanish in *La Jornada Semanal,* (Mexico City) October 8, 1995.

The Artist as Criminal first appeared in Spanish in *La Jornada* (Mexico City) and then in English translation in *The Drama Review,* 40:1, Spring 1996.

El Rey Del Cruce was originally a part of "The 1992 Trilogy." The complete performance script for this work was published as "1992: The Rediscovery of America" in *Warrior for Gringostroika* Graywolf Press, 1993.

DEDICATION/DEDICATORIA

ONE OF THE GREAT CONTRIBUTIONS OF EXPERIMENTAL ART, especially performance, over the past ten years has been the development of models of intercultural collaboration, and I've been both a co-creator and a beneficiary of these models. Most of my ideas and my performance work exist thanks to, and in relation to the work of dozens of accomplices who have been willing to cross many dangerous borders with me. They have risked their skin, their identity, and their dignity to contribute to a deeper and more complex understanding among races, cultures, and generations. These *locos* and *locas* have accompanied me to the most unlikely places (from Montana to Helsinki, and from the Basque country to Buenos Aires, and many conceptual countries in between) and at times they have faced real physical and political danger with me. Among others, they are:

Lorena Wolffer, *la chida one* aka *la Mae West del Centro Histórico*; Roberto Sifuentes, *el Cyber-Vato*; Rubén Martínez, *el Love-Vato*; Nola Mariano, *la doña*; Anastasia Herold, *la Húngara*; Elaine *la sesos* Katzenberger; Gustavo Vazquez, *el chueco*; Beto Arcos, *el jarocho*; James Luna; Nancy *co*-Jones; Kim Chan, *la china chola*; Cristina King; Joe Lambert; Amalia Mesa-Bains; Sara Shelton Mann; Richard Schechner; Roger Bartra; Iñigo Manglano-Ovalle; Juan Tejeda; Peter Sellars; Josefina Ramírez; Enrique Chagoya; Felipe Ehrenberg; René Yañez, *el capo*; Marco Vinicio González; Abel López; Encarnación Teruel; José Torres-Tama; Nao Bustamante; Cesar Martínez; Lorena Orozco; Elia Arce; Rogelio Villareal; Norma Medina; Carmel Kooros;

Josefina Alcazar; Michelle Ceballos; Rona Michele; Cynthia Wallis; Jeff Jones; Lynne Hershman; Branda Miller; Richard Lou and Robert Sánchez, *los antropolocos;* Andrea Suess; Silvana Straw; B. Stanley; Michelle Parkerson; Quique Aviles; and of course, of coursísimo, my dearísima mother Martha, *la Reina de Cocoteros*; and my beloved son Guillermo Emiliano, *el micro-brujo*; my rockero nephews Ricardiaco and Carlitos; and grandma Carmen and tíos Rubén y Eugenio, who all chose recently to leave this mad planet in search of permanent peace.

This book is dedicated to all of them. They have given me so much slack, unconditional tenderness, and chile power. They are always patient with my fuck-ups, they protect me from my formidable enemies, and they take very good care of my fourteen different selves. They certainly know the meaning of living right on the border, and the importance of transcultural friendship and collaboration — perhaps the only keys out of the mess we have gotten into.

Querida clica, los adoro, los venero, con ustedes, hasta la fuckin' muerte.

CONTENTS

INTRODUCTION

I AM A NOMADIC MEXICAN ARTIST/WRITER IN THE PROCESS OF Chicanization, which means I am slowly heading North. My journey not only goes from South to North, but from Spanish to Spanglish, and then to English; from ritual art to high-technology; from literature to performance art; and from a static sense of identity to a repertoire of multiple identities. Once I get "there," wherever it is, I am forever condemned to return, and then to obsessively reenact my journey. In a sense, I am a border Sisyphus.

This book describes my vision of a multicentric, hybrid American culture and my understanding of the United States' end-of-the-century identity crisis. The central questions running like bitter blood through the pages of this apparently eclectic collection are: What does it mean to be alive and to make art in an apocalyptic era framed/reframed by changing borders, ferocious racial violence, irrational fears of otherness and hybridity, spiritual emptiness, AIDS and other massively destructive diseases, ecological devastation, and, of course, lots of virtual space? How to function as a fluid border-crosser, intellectual "coyote," and intercultural diplomat in and around this abrupt landscape? And ultimately, how to understand the perils and advantages of living in a country that speaks at least ninety different languages and — unwillingly — hosts peoples from practically every nation, race, and religious creed on earth? In a sense, this book is a disnarrative ode to hybrid America — a new country in a new continent, yet to be named.

The texts and images collected here have been conceptually arranged, that is, they are meant to engage, expand, challenge, and reveal one another contextually. You could call this a kind of post-Mexican literary hypertext: The reader follows multidirectional links that connect throughout the book, emulating the endless journeys and border crossings which are at the core of my experience, and therefore my art. In fact, I encourage readers to create their own order for the material.

Since I don't believe in the existence of *linguas francas*, my choice not to translate (or to purposely mistranslate) the sections in Spanglish, Gringoñol, bad French, and indigenous languages is part of an aesthetic and a political strategy. I hope that this is apparent to the reader who, at times, will feel partially "excluded" from the work; but after all, partial exclusion is a quintessential contemporary experience, ¿que no? The "Glossary of Borderisms" at the end of the book contains some conceptual clues that might help when traveling across my performance continent.

I hope with all my heart that this book will contribute to the sorting out of the great crises of our times, and to the mapping of a more enlightened cartography for the next century. And I hope that despite its experimental nature, it won't become just another obscure text to be discussed by art theoreticians and cultural critics. It should speak to politicized artists, students, journalists, activists, teachers, techno-pirates, alternative rockeros, utopian thinkers, radical cultural organizers, anarchists, and border-crossers of all sorts — to anyone who is currently thinking out loud and fighting to recover the freedoms that our political and corporate classes have stolen from us so efficiently over the last fifteen years.

Perhaps in the very near future most of America's support systems for alternative culture will already have been dismembered by a myopic political milieu that sees no function for art in society. Maybe a new counterculture (via the Internet, 'zines, pirate radio, and

CD-ROMS) will have replaced the crumbling structures and broken networks. Perhaps my colleagues and I will be engaged in a very different aesthetic and political praxis. Maybe we'll be dead, mad, in jail, or exiled in another country. But I hope that the great project of redefinition of who we are — as a continent and as a people — will still be in progress, and that a new generation of *locos* and *locas* will continue the hard work.

For the moment, I offer the reader my thoughts, my performances, my broken symbols, my hybrid languages, my costumes, and my eclectic collection of masks.

Gómez-Peña
Mexico City, August 1995

Right: San Pocho Aztlaneca prepares to cut off his tongue in "The Temple of Confessions." Ex-Teresa Arte Alternativo, Mexico City, 1995. Photo by Monica Naranjo

THE NEW WORLD BORDER

FREEFALLING TOWARD A BORDERLESS FUTURE

*Performed live, voice filtered by delay effect; with a live simultaneous transla-
tion into French, Gringoñol, or Esperanto. Soundbed: A mix of Indian drums,
Gregorian chants, and occasional police sirens.*

      . . . per ipsum ecu nipsum, eti nipsum
      et T.Video Patri Omni-impotente
      per omnia saecula saeculeros
      I see
      I see
      I see a whole generation
      freefalling toward a borderless future
      incredible mixtures beyond science fiction:
          cholo-punks, pachuco krishnas,
          Irish concheros, butoh rappers, cyber-Aztecs,
          Gringofarians, Hopi rockers, y demás . . .
      I see them all
      wandering around
      a continent without a name
      the forgotten paisanos
      howling corridos in Fresno & Amarillo
      the Mixteco pilgrims
      heading North toward British Columbia
      the Australian surfers

waiting for the big wave at Valparaiso
the polyglot Papagos
waiting for the sign to return
the Salvadorans coming North (to forget)
the New Yorkers going South (to remember)
the stubborn Europeans in search of the last island
      — Zumpango, Cozumel, Martinique
I see them all
wandering around
a continent without a name
el TJ transvestite
translating Nuyorican versos in Univisión
the howling L.A. junkie
bashing NAFTA with a bullhorn
El Warrior for Gringostroika
scolding the First World on MTV
AIDS warriors reminding us all
of the true priorities in life
Lacandonian shamans
exorcising multinationals at dawn
yuppie tribes paralyzed by guilt & fear
grunge rockeros on the edge of a cliff
all passing through Califas
enroute to other selves
& other geographies
(I speak in tongues)
standing on the map of my political desires
I toast to a borderless future
(I raise my glass of wine toward the moon)
with . . .
our Alaskan hair
our Canadian head

our U.S. torso
our Mexican genitalia
our Central American cojones
our Caribbean sperm
our South American legs
our Patagonian feet
our Antarctic nails
jumping borders at ease
jumping borders with pleasure
amen, hey man

THE FREE TRADE ART AGREEMENT/
EL TRATADO DE LIBRE CULTURA

I AM A MIGRANT PERFORMANCE ARTIST. I WRITE IN AIRPLANES, TRAINS, and cafés. I travel from city to city, coast to coast, country to country, smuggling my work and the work and ideas of my colleagues. I collaborate with artists and writers from various communities and disciplines. We connect with groups who think like us, and debate with others who disagree. And then I carry the ideas elsewhere. Home is always somewhere else. Home is both "here" and "there" or somewhere in between. Sometimes it's nowhere.

I make art about the misunderstandings that take place at the border zone. But for me, the border is no longer located at any fixed geopolitical site. I carry the border with me, and I find new borders wherever I go.

I travel across a different America. My America is a continent (not a country) that is not described by the outlines on any of the standard maps. In my America, "West" and "North" are mere nostalgic abstractions — the South and the East have slipped into their mythical space. For example, Quebec seems closer to Latin America than to its Anglophone twin. My America includes different peoples, cities, borders, and nations. For instance, the Indian nations of Canada and the United States, and also the multiracial neighborhoods in the larger cities all seem more like Third World micro-republics than like communities that are part of some "western democracy." Today, the phrase "western democracy" seems hollow and quaint.

5

When I am on the East Coast of the United States, I am also in Europe, Africa, and the Caribbean. There, I like to visit Nuyo Rico, Cuba York, and other micro-republics. When I return to the U.S. Southwest, I am suddenly back in Mexamerica, a vast conceptual nation that also includes the northern states of Mexico, and overlaps with various Indian nations. When I visit Los Angeles or San Francisco, I am at the same time in Latin America and Asia. Los Angeles, like Mexico City, Tijuana, Miami, Chicago, and New York, is practically a hybrid nation/city in itself. Mysterious underground railroads connect all these places — syncretic art forms, polyglot poetry and music, and transnational pop cultures function as meridians of thought and axes of communication.

Here/there, the indigenous and the immigrant share the same space but are foreigners to each other. Here/there we are all potential border-crossers and cultural exiles. We have all been uprooted to different degrees, and for different reasons, but not everyone is aware of it. Here/there, homelessness, border culture, and deterritorialization are the dominant experience, not just fancy academic theories.

THE FOURTH WORLD & OTHER UTOPIAN CARTOGRAPHIES

The work of the artist is to force open the matrix of reality to introduce unsuspected possibilities. Artists and writers are currently involved in the redefinition of our continental topography. We see through the colonial map of North, Central, and South America, to a more complex system of overlapping, interlocking, and overlaid maps. Among others, we can see Amerindia, Afroamerica, Americamestiza-y-mulata, Hybridamerica, and Transamerica — the "other America" that belongs to the homeless, and to nomads, migrants, and exiles. We try to imagine more enlightened cartographies: a map of the Americas with no borders; a map turned upside down; or one in which the countries have borders that are organically drawn by geography, culture, and immigration, and not by the capricious hands of economic domination and political bravado.

Personally, I oppose the outdated fragmentation of the standard map of America with the conceptual map of Arte-America — a continent made of people, art, and ideas, not countries. When I perform, this map becomes my conceptual stage. Though no one needs a passport to enter my performance continent, the audience is asked to swallow their fears and to question any ethnocentric assumptions they might have about otherness, Mexico, Mexicans, other languages, and alternative art forms.

I oppose the sinister cartography of the New World Order with the conceptual map of the New World Border — a great trans- and intercontinental border zone, a place in which no centers remain. It's all margins, meaning there are no "others," or better said, the only true "others" are those who resist fusion, *mestizaje,* and cross-cultural dialogue. In this utopian cartography, hybridity is the dominant culture; Spanglish, Franglé, and Gringoñol are *linguas francas;* and monoculture is a culture of resistance practiced by a stubborn or scared minority.

I also oppose the old colonial dichotomy of First World/Third World with the more pertinent notion of the Fourth World — a conceptual place where the indigenous peoples meet with the diasporic communities. In the Fourth World, there is very little place for static identities, fixed nationalities, "pure" languages, or sacred cultural traditions. The members of the Fourth World live between and across various cultures, communities, and countries. And our identities are constantly being reshaped by this kaleidoscopic experience. The artists and writers who inhabit the Fourth World have a very important role: to elaborate the new set of myths, metaphors, and symbols that will locate us within all of these fluctuating cartographies.

THE FREE TRADE AGREEMENT

The North American Free Trade Agreement (NAFTA), signed by Canada, the United States, and Mexico, has created the largest artificial economic community on the planet. In terms of geography and

7

demographics, it is much larger than the European Union or the Pacific Rim. Sadly, out of all the possible trade agreements that could have been designed, the "neoliberal" version is not exactly an enlightened one. It is based on the arrogant fallacy that "the market" will solve any and all problems, and it avoids the most basic social, labor, environmental, and cultural responsibilities that are actually the core of any relationship between the three countries.

Many burning questions remain unanswered: Given the endemic lack of political and economic symmetry between the three participating countries, will Mexico become a mega-*maquiladora* [assembly plant] or, as Chicana artist Yareli Arismendi has stated, "the largest Indian reservation of the United States," or will it be treated as an equal by its bigger partners? Will the predatory Statue of Liberty devour the contemplative Virgin of Guadalupe, or will they merely dance a sweaty

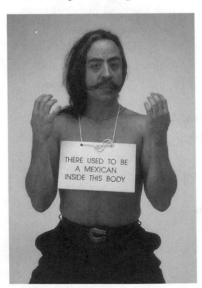

quebradita? Will Mexico become a toxic and cultural waste dump for its northern partners? Given the exponential increase of American trash- and media-culture in Mexico, what will happen to our indigenous traditions, our social and cultural rituals, our language, and national psyche? Will Mexico's future generations become hyphenated Mexican-Americans, brown-skinned gringos, or Canochis (upside-down Chicanos)? And what about our Anglo partners? Will they slowly become Chica-nadians, Waspbacks, Gringotlanis, and Anglomalans ?

Whatever the answers are, NAFTA will profoundly affect our lives in many ways. Whether we like it or not, a new era has begun, and a new economic and cultural topography has been designed for us. We must now find our new place and role within this bizarre Federation of U.S. Republics.

THE FREE ART AGREEMENT

Artists are talking about the need to create a structure parallel to NAFTA — a kind of Free Art Agreement — for the exchange of ideas and noncommercial artwork, not just consumer goods and hollow dreams. If formed, the task of this network of thinkers, artists, and arts organizations from Mexico, the United States, and Canada (and why not the Carribean?) would be to develop models of cross-cultural dialogue and interdisciplinary artistic collaboration. Through multilingual publications, radio, film, video, and performance collaborations, more complex and mutable notions of "North American" cultures and identities could be conceived.

Of course, in the signing of this new transcultural contract, it would be fundamental to address relationships of power and assumptions about privilege among the participating artists, communities, and countries. A willingness to cross borders and good intentions are not enough. Crossing the border from North to South has very different implications than crossing the same border from South to North; the border cannot possibly mean the same to a tourist as it does to an undocumented worker. People with social, racial, or economic privilege have an easier time crossing physical borders, but they have a much harder time negotiating the invisible borders of culture and race.

"Transculture" and hybridity have different connotations for a person of color than for an Anglo American. In the conflictive history of the North/South dialogue and the multicultural debate, Americans and Europeans have often performed involuntary colonialist roles. In their desire to help, they often unknowingly become ventriloquists, impresarios, *flaneurs,* messiahs, or cultural transvestites. Though painful, these forms of benign colonialism must be discussed openly, but without accusing anyone. The objective is to replace these problematic relation-ships with more enlightened ones, not to scare or punish potential allies. In order to rebuild broken alliances and regain lost trust, there must be a new commitment. As Canadian artist Chris Creighton Kelly says, "Anglo Americans must finally go beyond tolerance, sacrifice, and moral reward. Their commitment to cultural equity must become a way of being in the world." In exchange, we artists "of color" will have to acknowledge their efforts, slowly bring our guard down, change the strident tone of our discourse, and begin another heroic project — that of forgiving, and therefore healing our colonial and post–colonial wounds. *Ojo por ojo; diente por diente.*

GLOBAL TRANSCULTURE VS. NEONATIONALISM

Today, wherever we turn, we witness a nasty wrestling match between a global consumer transculture and the resurgence of virulent ultranationalisms. The masterminds of the New World Order insist that the media, computer communications, cyber-space, and the global econ-omy have already created a single, borderless world community. They speak of "total culture" and "total television," a grandiose pseudo-inter-nationalist world view à la CNN that creates the illusion of immediacy, simultaneity, and sameness, thereby numbing our political will and homogenizing our identities.

Pop culture is full of revealing examples. The depoliticized World Beat and New Age movements, and the Third World adventures of David Byrne and Paul Simon seem to be telling us that there is a gen-tle way out of our race, class, and nationality; that we can all be friends within the safe and neutral space of poly-ethnic music, weekend medi-tation seminars, and "primitive" memorabilia.

This phenomenon is also evident in the contemporary art world. Los Angeles poet Rubén Martínez warns us to examine the hype of "free trade art" — a fin de siecle initiative promoted by the major cultural institutions in all three NAFTA countries. Its objective: to use art as a form of conservative diplomacy, and to create a conflict-free image for a country in order to seduce investors and promote cultural tourism. Free trade art is tricky. It promotes transculture and celebrates border crossings, but for all the wrong reasons. Despite their cross-cultural rhetoric, the NAFTArt impresarios would rather bypass the dangerous border zone, with its minefields of race and gender, and its political geysers. They literally cross the border in helicopters, and prefer to deal directly with what they perceive as "the center" (New York, Los Angeles, Toronto, or Mexico City). Unfortunately, they are trying to ignore — or don't want to accept — the fact that contemporary culture has already been completely decentralized; in fact, the old centers are now being reconquered by the margins.

In reaction to the transculture imposed from above, a new essentialist culture is emerging, one that advocates national, ethnic, and gender separatism in the quest for cultural autonomy, "bio-regional identity," and "traditional values." This tendency to overstate difference, and the unwillingness to change or exchange, is a product of communities in turmoil who, as an antidote to the present confusion, have chosen to retreat to the fictional womb of their own separate histories. Even our so-called "progressive" communities are retrenching to a fundamentalist stance.

We know why: The end of the century breeds *horror vacui:* multiculturalism has gone sour; racism and sexism are still rampant; and immigrants and people of color are being blamed for all social ills. But there is a better alternative to the obvious choice between ultranationalisms and a homogenized global culture: a grassroots cultural response that understands the contextual and strategic value of nationalism, as well as the importance of crossing borders and establishing cross-cultural alliances.

THE HYBRID

I wish to propose a third alternative: the hybrid — a cultural, political, aesthetic, and sexual hybrid. My version of the hybrid is cross-racial, polylinguistic, and multicontexual. From a disadvantaged position, the hybrid expropriates elements from all sides to create more open and fluid systems. Hybrid culture is community-based yet experimental, radical but not static or dogmatic. It fuses "low" and "high" art, primitive and high-tech, the problematic notions of self and other, the liquid entities of North and South, East and West.

An ability to understand the hybrid nature of culture develops from an experience of dealing with a dominant culture from the outside. The artist who understands and practices hybridity in this way can be at the same time an insider and an outsider, an expert in border crossings, a temporary member of multiple communities, a citizen of two or more nations. S/he performs multiple roles in multiple contexts. At times s/he can operate as a cross-cultural diplomat, as an intellectual *coyote* (smuggler of ideas) or a media pirate. At other times, s/he assumes the role of nomadic chronicler, intercultural translator, or political trickster. S/he speaks from more than one perspective, to more than one community, about more than one reality. His/her job is to trespass, bridge, interconnect, reinterpret, remap, and redefine; to find the outer limits of his/her culture and cross them.

The prescence of the hybrid denounces the faults, prejudices, and fears manufactured by the self-proclaimed center, and threatens the very raison d'etre of any monoculture, official or not. It reminds us that we are not the product of just one culture; that we have multiple and transitional identities; that we contain a multiplicity of voices and selves, some of which may even be contradictory. And it tells us that there is nothing wrong with contradiction.

Perhaps the main obstacle that the hybrid must face is the mistrust of both the official transculture and the separatist cultures of resistance. Also, precisely because of its elasticity and open nature, the hybrid model can be appropriated by anyone to mean practically anything. Since the essence of its borders is oscillation, these boundaries can be conveniently repositioned to include or exclude different peoples and

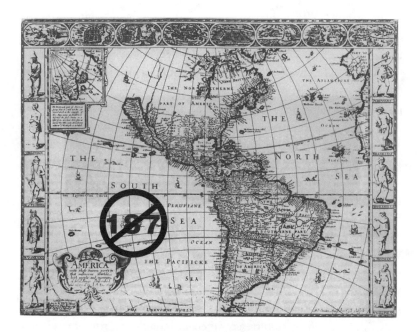

communities. Eventually, even the official transculture will appropriate the hybrid to baptize free-trade art festivals, boring academic conferences, and glossy publications. Once the hybrid model is depoliticized, we will have to look for another paradigm and a new set of metaphors to explain the complexities and dangers of the times.

THE COLUMBIAN LEGACY OF DIVISIVENESS

The borders keep multiplying. It just doesn't cut it anymore to pretend that the enemy is always outside. The separatist, sexist, racist, and authoritarian tendencies that we condemn others for perpetrating also exist within our own communities and within our own individual selves. We can't continue to hide behind the pretext that "straight, white men," or the all purpose "dominant culture" are the source of all our problems. Every community must face this fact: Dominance is contextual. We all, at different times and in different contexts, enjoy some privileges over other people and perform the ever-changing roles of victim and victimizer, exploited and exploiter, colonizer and colonized.

We must now have the courage to turn our gaze inward and begin to raise the touchy issues that most of us avoided in the past. Some examples: Men of color are active protagonists in the history of sexism, and Anglo-American women share the blame in the history of racism. African Americans and Afro-Carribbeans often have a hard time getting along. U.S.-born Latinos and Latin Americans cannot fully understand one another — despite our cultural similarities, we are separated by invisible, idiosyncratic borders, and our political and cultural agendas are quite different. Latinos and Afro-Americans can be as racist toward one another as the "dominant culture" is toward both of us. No one is immune to the virus of internalized colonialism. Third World feminists and American feminists still haven't reached a basic agreement regarding priorities and strategies. The "boys club" artists of the '60s and '70s can hardly be in the same room with the multiracial and multisexual artists of the '80s and '90s. Many of these embittered veterans resent the "irreverence" and "ungratefulness" of the younger artists, and also the intensity and directness of the women. In fact, most straight men are still irritated when sexism is mentioned at all. My women friends have consistently pointed out the hypocrisy of my hiding behind ethnicity to avoid gender issues.

The art world is a dysfunctional family — a micro-universe reflecting the larger society. Artists and academicians rarely talk to one another. "Community artists" and politicized artists who work within major institutions still see each other as enemies, not as allies working on different fronts. Artists who work directly with troubled communities, such as the homeless, prisoners, migrant workers, or inner-city youth are viewed as opportunists, and their intentions are constantly called into question. "Successful" artists of color are perceived as having been "co-opted," or as "sell-outs." Those who venture into theory are accused of being elitists, not "organic" in relation to their community. The absurd premise behind this belief is that if we are truly committed to our communities, we must be marginal, poor, angry, and anti-intellectual. Both Anglo American liberals and essentialists of color are still immersed in Byzantine debates about who is "authentic" and who isn't. And the impresarios of contemporary art are always ready to evaluate the degree of authenticity of their newly discovered "primitives." Artists who favor hybridity and cross-cultural collaboration are viewed with mistrust by all sides.

Well-meaning liberals often commit an insidious form of racism though they have learned the correct terminology to avoid offense, they remain unwilling to give up their control and stop running the show. Many white multiculturalists are currently experiencing an acute case of "compassion fatigue," and they are either bailing out for good, or retrenching to pre–multicultural stances. Their thin commitment to cultural equity evaporates before our very eyes. Many alternative art spaces have replaced their "multicultural" programs of the early '90s with "exciting new trends" (interactive technologies, eco-art, and neotribalism, among others). Since multiculturalism was never understood as part of a larger political project — the creation of a multiparticipatory society — but as a mere art trend, these alternative spaces see nothing wrong with the lack of continuity in their interests. In fact, the U.S. art world, obsessed as it is with novelty and surprise, nurtures this lack of continuity.

Today, in the '90s, our communities are ferociously divided by gender, race, class, and age. An abyss — not a borderline — separates us from our children, our teenagers, and our elders. The Columbian legacy of divisiveness is more present than ever. This is contemporary America: a land of diversity where no one tolerates difference; a land of bizarre eclecticism where everyone must know their place. Here, artists and activists spend more time competing for attention and funding than establishing coalitions with other individuals and groups.

Chicano theoretician Tomas Ybarra-Frausto suggests that, "we must resist all attempts at intercultural warfare," and I completely agree. In order to begin the great project of racial, gender, and generational reconciliation that America so badly needs, we must demand a cease-fire and sign a temporary peace treaty. Perhaps the key here is the recognition that we all are partially guilty and equally disenfranchised. At least among ourselves, as in a family reunion, we must face these issues directly but with respect, without indicting anyone, without name-calling. Our cultural institutions can perform an important role: they can function as experimental laboratories to develop and test new models of collaboration between races, genders, and generations, and as "free zones" for intercultural dialogue, radical thinking, and community-building.

DYSFUNCTIONAL COMMUNITIES

Our "ethnic"communities have changed so dramatically in the past ten years that they might no longer be just "ours." Our neighborhoods and barrios have become much more multiracial and impoverished. Our families, schools and community centers are falling appart. Interracial violence, police brutality, homelessness, AIDS, and drugs have increased exponentially. It becomes increasingly hard to differentiate between the South Bronx and Soweto; between South Central Los Angeles or South Chicago and the São Paolo *favelas.* Our outdated social theories have been rendered inadequate by these changes; and artists and activists have become foreigners and exiles in our own communities.

Despite the fact that in the '90s the word "community" has taken on myriad meanings (most of which are open-ended and ever-changing), some people still utilize the demagogic banner of "the (mythical and unified) community" to infuse their actions with moral substance. They attack and exclude others who express different views on racial identity, sexuality, or aesthetics, and resent the newly arrived immigrants: "I represent my community. S/he doesn't." "His community doesn't back him anymore." "This art is not community-based." And so on. Not only does this widen already existing divisions, but it provides the media and the conservative institutions with the awaited confirmation of their stereotype: that artists and activists of color who are demanding change simply can't get along.

In the current fog of confusion, one thing is clear: We must rediscover our communities in turmoil, redefine our problematic relationship to them, and find new ways to serve them. And those who choose, for whatever reasons, never to go back to their original communities must be respected. No one has the moral right to question their decision. Clearly, we need artists working on all fronts and in all sectors of society, both in dominant and alternative institutions.

The art world is a particularly strange community, in that it has no elders or children. Elders are ignored and children are seen as a nuisance. This is a microscopic expression of the dehumanization of the larger society. Latino leaders insist that everything we think and do in the future must be shared with other generations. We must invite our elders, teenagers, and young children to the table and reconnect with them, for they can remind us of the truly important things in life. We must bridge this grave generational gap and ensure that when we leave the table, others will take our place.

The teenagers' situation is particularly sensitive. They rightfully believe that we are partially responsible for the dangerous world they are inheriting. They see us as inefficient and intransigent, and they have a point. We must learn to accept responsibility and seek more effective languages to communicate with them. Teenagers have tremendous things to teach us: They have fewer hang-ups about race and gender, they are much more at ease with crisis and hybridity, and they understand our cities and neighborhoods better than we do. In fact, if there is an art form that truly speaks for the present crisis of our communities, this form is rap.

THE GREAT COLLABORATIVE PROJECT

The indigenous philosophies of the Americas remind us that everything is interconnected, all destructive and divisive forces have the same source, and all struggles for the respect of life, in all its variants, lead in the same direction.

The great project of reform and reconciliation must be, above all, a collaborative one, and all concerned communities must take part in it. According to Native American prophecy, we are in the era of the seventh generation, and we all need to begin sharing our secrets, skills, strategies, and infrastructures. It's about time that politicians, the media, and civic and corporate leaders begin to take note: No effective solution to the multiple crises that afflict contemporary American society can be implemented without the consent and direct participation of each of these overlapping communities. My colleagues and I politely ask you to join in.

the new world border

If I had known, I wouldn't have gone.

—Columbus

When the world was ours, you took it away from us.
When the world was yours, you didn't want to share it.
Now that the world is ours again
you are trying to dress & act like we do.
What's wrong with you Teules?

—Moctezuma Jr.

Everything is changing & moving so fast that we don't have
time to confront our immediate past. Soon everything will be new.

—East German psychiatrist

No one or everyone should be named.

—Moira Roth

Fresh water from Canada,
and cheap oil from Mexico,
all served in an American glass,
the perfect Free Trade Cocktail, ¡caramba!

—Fictional ad by the NAFTA Commission

Too much (concept); and too little (movement).

—The Washington Post

Gómez-Peña: How would you define Los Angeles?
Bob Wisdom: It could be Beirut. It could be utopia.
We'll know next weekend.

THE NEW WORLD BORDER:
Prophecies for the End of the Century

THE NEW WORLD BORDER WAS OFTEN DESCRIBED BY COLLEAGUES and journalists as "chicano cyber-punk art" and at one point (though many essentialist Chicanos still have a hard time considering me a Chicano) I chose to embrace the definition. In this language-based and highly technified epic performance, I decided to push my border aesthetics (layering and clashing of languages, musical styles, sounds, and images) to an extreme. My collaborators and I used four sources of prerecorded and live sound, as well as state-of-the-art technology to mix and filter our voices. We spoke in Spanish, French, English, Spanglish, Franglé, and several made up "robo-languages." The "simultaneous translations" were purposely incorrect. The idea was to force the audience to experience the cultural vertigo of living in a multilingual/multiracial society.

In the NWB, the processes of balkanization that Eastern Europe underwent from 1989 to 1992 are projected onto the United States: dozens of micro-republics pop up everywhere; the U.S.-Mexico border disappears; Spanglish becomes the "official" language; the hybrid state is now a political reality; and the ethnic/social pyramid has been turned upside down.

There is really no plot, nor recognizable "characters." The performers on stage are mere media images and virtual reality clones of our own (fictionalized) identities. Their voices are disembodied, and their/our actions have become totally ritualized and antitheatrical.

Of all my "proscenium pieces," perhaps the NWB has engendered the most contradictory and extreme responses from critics and audience members. Before the performances, we often utilized the strategy of "segregating" the audience according to racial and/or linguistic criteria, and people had a very hard time feeling like a minority in their own country, even if only for an hour and a half. But perhaps what created the most controversy was the use of dead chickens hanging onstage as a metaphor for violence toward Mexicans. We were often visited by animal rights activists who objected to our "violent actions toward the chickens" and vehemently accused us of "desecrating animals" for art's sake. Once, they went to the extent of equating "violence to animals with violence to Mexicans." In all cases, we were defended by audience members who told the animal rights people that they wished "to discuss more important issues."

Sometimes performed as a solo, and other times as a duet (first with Coco Fusco, and later with Roberto Sifuentes), the NWB toured extensively for two years throughout the United States, Canada, Europe, and Latin America, and was performed as part of various international festivals and biennales. Every performance was different. In each city — and country — the piece was redesigned to incorporate cultural and political specificities of the site. This script (as performed by myself and Roberto Sifuentes) is one of at least twenty-five different versions.

CHARACTERS:

GÓMEZ-PEÑA as *EL AZTEC HIGH-TECH*

Costume: Ritual makeup, mariachi suit, pachuco hat, skull earrings, Aztec chest piece, snakeskin boots, 3-D glasses, low-rider glasses, bandana, black gloves, heavy-metal bracelets, and an assortment of masks and wigs.

ROBERTO SIFUENTES as *SUPER-POCHO*

Costume: Black suit, shirt & tie, mariachi hat, pre-Columbian–style facial and arm tattoos, wrestler mask, "caucasian" mask, death mask, stereotypical "low-rider" outfit.

OPTIONAL PRE–PERFORMANCE EVENT IN THE LOBBY:

Super-Pocho and El Aztec High-Tech enter the theater on their knees. They get up and walk around the lobby with a basket, collecting objects from the audience:

Is there anything you would like to give away? Anything you don't really need? Money, IDs, condoms, keys, a poem, a credit card, your pain, your anger? Just be sure you don't need what you're parting with to face the end of the twentieth century.

SET DESIGN:

A bizarre radio studio somewhere in the immediate future. The feeling of the space is ceremonial. A lectern stands stage left. A human skeleton hangs center stage, Christlike. Various dead chickens hang from the ceiling at different heights. There is a chair downstage right, and next to it is a small table for props. A portable tape player plays "radiorama" programs in different languages. A semicircle of candles separates the stage from the audience.

ONCE THE AUDIENCE IS SEATED, ALL HOUSE AND STAGE LIGHTS GO OUT.

Gómez-Peña walks onstage, looking angry. He stares intently at various audience members, then he suddenly begins doing hare krishna chants in Spanglish. He turns on the tape player and sits down in the chair. He speaks in tongues, mixed with corporate words.

Roberto Sifuentes stands motionless behind the lectern, wearing a wrestler mask and a mariachi hat.

GP/VOICE GOES FROM NORMAL TO SATANIC:

I'm sorry. I'm having an identity crisis on stage . . .

De Volada Productions presenta un live broadcast from (name of the city where the performance takes place) on (date of the actual performance). Miento. This is not a performance, but a cue-to-cue rehearsal. Miento. This is an authentic Indian ritual. Miento. This is a techno-town meeting. Fuck it! This is what it is. ¡Chingao!

Hey man, pay attention, the other is talking to you; the Mexican beast has come to get even . . .

Now, let's see how far we can go tonight with only six chickens, one ghetto blaster, three mikes, a cheesy voice mixer, a real human skeleton, and a bunch of trinkets bought in La Merced Market and Canal Street. *(he howls)*

PROPHECY #I: THE FIN DE SIECLE SOCIETY

MUSIC: CHICANO RAP

GP/LOW-RIDER/DISC-JOCKEY VOICE, SUAVECITO & BREATHY:

Hello queridos yuppies, turistas, voyeuristas, antropólogos aficionados, perplexed citizens of the end of the century. This is the voice of El Aztec High-Tech broadcasting from the heights of WXYZ-FM, 93 megahertz above reality.

I'm the representative of the Liberated Republic of Aztlán in the signing of an Accord du Free Cultura among the artistas/activistas of the New World Border, ¿que no?

I'm here with Super-Pocho Dos, el vato más loco de Pacoima, in a promotional tour across the Americas.

I warn you. This ain't performance art but pure Chicano science fiction. Anygüeyes, comenzamos sin translation cha-cha!

Y ahora, nuestro corresponsal en los Estamos Hundidos . . .

MUSIC: ROCK BY CHILEAN GROUP *LOS ELECTRODOMESTICOS*

GP walks toward chicken #3, then back toward skeleton, mouthing a painful shout.

RS/ANCHORMAN VOICE (WITH ECHO):

Imagine a new American continent without borders. It's a continent that has become a huge border zone. Think of it as the New World Border.

We are living in the age of pus-modernity, a blistering, festering present. And in these times, all known political systems and economic structures are dysfunctional. They are being reformed, replaced, or destroyed. Many see this as the era of la desmodernidad, a term that comes from the Mexican noun *desmadre,* which can mean either having no mother, or living in chaos. The Great Fiction of a social order has evaporated and has left us in a state of meta-orphanhood. We are all, finally, untranslatable hijos de la chingada.

GP/FRENCH ACCENT:

Les enfants de la chingada da-da.

MUSIC: RECORDED CHANTS IN QUECHUA

As GP addresses the hanging chicken, RS counts backward from 10 to 0.

GP/DRAMATIC & SLOW:

(to the chicken) Yes, we are linked by imaginary networks . . . (10) members of a fictional society, no longer defined by ethnicity, ideology, nationality, or language, but by time. (9)

Yes, the only recognizable parameters of this emerging society are "ruptures," such as the fall of the Berlin Wall, the Baghdad genocide, the L.A. insurrection . . . the return of xenophobia. (8)

Yes, I roam around this shattered puzzle in state of acute apendejamiento (7) (from the noun *pendejo,* o sea, stupid; and the verb *mentir,* meaning to lie).

Yes, I'm lying to you, extranjero en tu propio pais. (6)

No, we don't lie together. In the end, we never lie together, vecinos abismales (5) still undiscovered to one another . . . el othercide, el otrocidio, (4) digo, the murdering of otherness. (3)

Es triste, tristísimo. Five hundred years later, Columbus and Queen Anacaona (2) still cannot understand each other, each mother, each madre (1) que fuckin' desmadre; tu honorificentia populi nostri. (0)

MUSIC STOPS.

GP/RADIO EVANGELIST VOICE (INTO MEGAPHONE):

Is this utopia or dystopia? Are we closer to Catholic heaven or capitalist hell? Is this re-a-li-ty or performance? Can anyone answer?! Can anyone tell me which country we are in? *(screaming)* I can't hear you!! I can't hear you!!

RS/AIRLINE HOSTESS VOICE (OVERLAPPING WITH GP):

Can anyone answer? Can anyone answer? *(continues repeating question every seven seconds into next text)*

GP/NASAL, OLD-FASHIONED MEXICAN RADIO VOICE:

Y lo peor del asunto es que Godzilla y El Santo are nowhere to be found, nowhere to be found, nowhere to be found . . .

BLACKOUT.

GP goes back to his chair.

MUSIC: "HONKY TANGO" BY ARGENTINE EXPERIMENTAL GROUP *LES LUTIERS*

PROPHECY #II: LA GRINGOSTROIKA

GP puts on holographic glasses and changes his Aztec headdress for a pachuco hat.

GP/NASAL, NERVOUS, AND VERY FAST:

In the wake of the stormy changes in the ex-Soviet bloc, the winds of gringostroika have reached every corner of our continent. Can we still call it "ours"? Who are "we" anyway?

Geopolitical borders have faded away. Due to the implementation of a Free Raid Agreement, and the creation of an untranslatable Zona de Libre Cogercio, the nations formerly known as Canada, the United States, and Mexico have merged painlessly to create the new Federation of U.S. Republics.

F.U.S.R. is controlled by a Master Chamber of Commerce, a Department of Transnational Tourism, and a Media Junta. The role of the presidents is now restricted to public relations, and the role of the military has been reduced to guarding banks, TV stations, and art schools. ¡No se me asuste güey!

The immediate effects of this integration are spectacular: The monocultural territories of the disbanded United States, commonly known as Gringolandia, have become drastically impoverished, leading to massive migrations of unemployed waspbacks to the South. All major metropolises have been fully borderized. In fact, there are no longer any visible cultural differences between Toronto, Manhattan, Chicago, Lost Angeles, or México Cida. They all look like downtown Tijuana on a Saturday night.

SLOWLY TURNS INTO DRUNKEN VOICE:

The First World/Third World geopolitical distinctions, vestiges of an outdated colonialist vocabulary, have completely overlapped.

The legendary U.S.-Mexico borderline, affectionately known as "The Tortilla Curtain," no longer exists. Pieces of the great Tortilla are now sentimental souvenirs hanging on the bedroom walls of idiotic tourists, like you.

The hundreds of thousands of Mexican POWs imprisoned for jaywalking in the Southwest have finally been released. Some of them now occupy important government positions. Acá servidor Gran Vato Charrollero perfor-meándose en ustedes *(pause)* . . . just kiddin'. Imagine this blackout, ¿suave?. . . Blackout!

BLACKOUT.

RS/REDNECK VOICE:

Hey man, cut this political mumbo jumbo. Do all Mexkins talk like this?

LIGHTS COME UP.

The following text is spoken by GP & RS simultaneously:

GP/THICK LATINO ACCENT:

(wearing a big smile and clearing his throat) Please check my pronunciation. Spanglish and Gringoñol have been proclaimed official languages, linguas francas. The controversial Spanglish Only Initiative that outlawed the use of English in the Southwest in 1992 spread quickly throughout the entire Federation. It's mind-blowing. Televisa, CNN, and CBC have joined to create Reali-TV, the largest media empire on the planet, in charge of broadcasting the daily New World Orders. Their slogan is "TV or not TV, that is the question!" And as if this weren't enough, United, American, and Continental Airlines have given up their hegemony to new and more chingonometric companies, such as Mexicanada Airlines and the amazing Alaskan-Patagonian Shuttle. . . . Are there any questions?

RS/GRINGO ACCENT (MISTRANSLATING):

El spanglish y el gringoñol han sido proclamados lenguas oficiales, linguas francas. La controversial Spanglish Only Iniciativa que en 1992 prohibió el uso del inglés en el Southwest, se extendió rápidamente por toda la federación. Es mind-blowing. Televisa, CNN, y CBC se han unido para crear Reali-TV, el imperio de los medios de comunicación más grande del planeta, a cargo de transmitir los New World Orders cada día. Su eslogan es "TV or not TV, esa es la pregunta." Y como si esto fuera poco, las líneas aéreas de United, American, and Continental cedieron su hegemonía a compañías mas nuevas y chingonométricas como Mexicanada de Aviación y el sorprendenti Alaskan-Patagonian Shuttle. . . . Hay alguna pregunta?

RS makes fart noises as the soundbed for next text.

GP/SLOW, DRUNKEN VOICE:
Ay! . . . Reality looks and feels like a cyber-punk film codirected by José Martí and Ted Turner on acid; and I, little post-Mexican romantic with my permanent poetical erection, cannot help but to ask out loud: Are we closer than ever to Art-mageddon or are we merely experiencing the birth pains of the new milennia?

RS: Shut up, you chicanocentric pedero! You intellectual drive-by shooter, you theoretical minority! . . . *(his tone becomes apologetic)* Sorry, this pirate radio broadcast has been authorized by the Department of Transnational Tourism. Whiteout please!

BLACKOUT.

PROPHECY #III: NEONATIONALISM

RS walks down center stage to a table, takes off his wrestler mask, and prepares a free-trade molotov cocktail, while chanting:
New World Order, New Disorder, New World Order, Free Trade Art, Utopia, Utopia, 93 . . . *(in loop)*

The bomb doesn't work. RS walks away, disappointed.

MUSIC: GERMAN BAND *POPOL VUH*

GP speaks into a megaphone in fascist-sounding tongues. He wears his "Warrior for Gringostroika" wrestling mask.

GP/ULTRAMILITANT VOICE (WITH REVERB):

We witness a resurgence of ultranationalist movements, together with the rise of the New World Border globalist rhetoric. Quebec, Puerto Rico, Aztlán, South Central Los Angeles, Yucatán, Panamá, and all the Indian Nations have seceded from the new Federation of U.S. Republics. Independent micro-republics are popping up everywhere in the blink of an eye. Verbigratia: *(he raises his right fist)* The twin cities of San Dollariego and Tijuana have united to form the Maquiladora Republic of San Diejuana. Hong Kong has relocated to Baja California to constitute the powerful Baja-Kong, the world's greatest producer of porn & tourist kitsch. The cities of Lost Angeles and Tokyo now share a corporate government called Japangeles, which oversees all the financial operations of the Pacific Rim. The Republik of Berkeley is the only Marxist-Leninist nation left on the globe. The Caribbean populations of the East Coast, including Nuyo Rico and Cuba York, have merged to form the Independent Pan-Carib Nation. They willingly accept refugees from Haiti and Miami. Florida and Cuba now share a corporate junta that has the cryptic name of "Lenin, Mas Canosa & Associates." The nation/city of Mexico D.F. (Detritus Defecalis), now called Tesmogtitlán (from the Náhuatl nouns *tesmog,* pollution, and *titlán,* place), with its fifty million inhabitants and its eight hundred square miles is presently negotiating its independence from the F.U.S.R. . . .

GP & RS/WHISPERING:
F.U.S.R. . . . F.U.S.R. . . . F.U.S.R. . . .

SOUND OF CLOCK TICKING.

ORIGINAL Gomez-Peña 1993 auf dem Titel der MORGENPOST-Bei-lage zum Sommertheater.

KOPIE Die „Walpurgisnachtmeute" 1995 in Kresniks „Gründ-gens" im Schauspielhaus.

Ertappt! Kresnik hat bei Peña abgekupfert

A German performance artist plagiarizes Gómez-Peña. Which of the two is more authentic? From the German newspaper *Hamburger Morgenpost,* April 11, 1995.

RS/REDNECK VOICE:

If you ungrateful greasers don't like it here, why don't you go back where you came from?

GP & RS put on their "Caucasian" masks. RS begins text in French. GP trans-lates simultaneously into English with a French accent.

RS/ACADEMIC VOICE:

Le mois dernier, le conference historique sur la paix multiculturelle s'est passé dans plusieurs villes de la Frontiere du Nouveau Monde. Toutes les villes ont été connectés par la tecnologie du video-satellite. L'objectif était de commencer le processus douloureux de resoudre les resentiments inter-etnique et la hysterie qui ont été crée par le gringostroika. Quatre principes importants ont été etablis. Je cite verbatim:

GP/FRENCH ACCENT:

Last month, the historical Multicultural Peace Conference took place simultaneously in numerous cities of the New World Border, all interactively connected through video-satellite technology. The objective was to begin the painful process of working out the interethnic resentments and cross-cultural hysteria created by gringostroika. Four important principles were established. I quote verbatim:

GP goes to center stage, positions a soccer ball, and threatens to kick it into the audience four times while subvocalizing RS's following text.

RS/COMPUTER VOICE:

1) No nation, community, or individual can claim racial, sexual, or aesthetic purity.

2) Beginning in January of 1995, all borders on the American continent will be open. No passport will be required.

3) All nations will operate with only one currency: the mighty peso.

4) Members of mono-racial minorities of European descent must be granted equal rights, voting power, and a free multicultural education.

RS/FRENCH NEWSCASTER VOICE:

On a demandé a tous les membres de F.U.S.R. d'implementer ces principes ipso facto. Ceux qui ne veulent pas accepter les regles suffriront un blocage économique. Magister dixit, Reali-TV, caput!

GP/FRENCH ACCENT (TRANSLATING SIMULTANEOUSLY):

All members of the F.U.S.R. have been asked to implement these principles immediately. Those who do not comply will be punished with embargo. Magister dixit, Reali-TV, caput!

BLACKOUT.

RS/COMPUTER VOICE:

Before we continue with this broadcast, I want everyone to repeat after me: "This is art. *(pause)* This is not reality. *(pause)* . . . Come on, let's hear it! *(the audience follows instructions)* Thank you. Gracias. Danke shöen.

PROPHECY #IV: THE MELTING PLOT VS. THE MENUDO CHOWDER

Seated on chair, GP drinks from a rubber heart and changes eyeglasses. RS puts on a blond wig and freezes in shame.

MUSIC. BRITISH-HINDU RAP BY *APACHI INDIAN*

GP changes accents abruptly during following text:

GP/PACHUCO ACCENT:

Hello raza. This is the voice of Gran Vato Charrollero interrupting your coitus as always. Tonight's broadcast is about migration . . . my-gration!

NASAL ACCENT:

This new society is characterized by mass migrations and bizarre interracial relations. As a result, new hybrid identities are emerging. All Mexican citizens have turned into Chicanos or Mexkimos, and all Canadians have become Chicanadians.

TEXAN ACCENT:

Everyone is now a borderígena, meaning a native of the great border region. According to *Transnational Geographic Magazine,* 70 percent of the population in the New World Border is undocumented, and up to 90 percent can be technically considered mesti-mulata, that is, the product of at least four racial mixtures.

THICK LATINO ACCENT:

Such is the case of the crazy Chicarricuas, who are the products of Puerto Rican–mulatto and Chicano–mestizo parents; and also the innumerable Germanchurians who descend from the union of West Germans and Manchurian Chinese.

CANTINFLAS VOICE:

When a Chicarricua marries a Hasidic Jew their child is called Hasidic vato loco. And when a displaced Belgian marries a Chicano, the offspring is called Belga-chica, which loosely translates as "little winnie."

Among the other significantly large half-breed groups are the Anglomalans, the Afro-Croatians, and the Jap-talians, many of whom I see here tonight. It's lovely and very, very post-Columbian, Culombian, may I say, say . . . melting plot.

MUSIC: SHAMANIC YODELING FROM PANAMÁ

GP walks back and forth from the skeleton to a chicken. When he is in front of a hanging chicken, he screams loudly as if he were being tortured.

RS/(W/ECHO):

(he wears headphones) Testing, testing . . . We've replaced the bankrupt notion of the melting plot with a model that is more germane to the times, that of the menudo chowder. According to this model, most of the ingredients do melt, but some stubborn chunks are condemned merely to float.

The Euro-Americans who resisted interracial love became a nomadic minority and eventually ended up migrating south to work for maquiladoras and fast-food restaurants. They get paid less than 200 pesos an hour. They are derogatively referred to as waspanos, waspitos, wasperos, or waspbacks. The basic rights of these downtrodden people are constantly violated, and there is no embassy to defend them.

This alarming "Anglophobia" is based on an absolute fallacy — that "they" have come to take "our" jobs. But the truth is that no hybrid in his or her right mind, including me, would work for such lousy wages.

GP/DRUGGIE VOICE:

(addresses the chicken) Ay, your past is gone for good; my past is gone for good . . . help me! Estoy perdido . . .

RS: *(interrupting)* Translation please!

GP: . . . al norte de un sur inexistente. Me captas cavernícola, ¿mex-plico?

RS: Translation please!

GP makes neanderthal sounds.

RS: *(angry)* Translation please!!

GP: Okay, okay. Lección de español numero cinco for advanced English speakers. . . . Falsa democracia?

RS: Translation please!

Members of the audience begin to answer.

GP: Sexual democracia?

RS: Translation please!

GP: U.S.A. te usa . . .

RS: Translation please!

GP: Censura no es cultura . . .

RS: Translation please!

GP: No. Censura no escultura . . .

RS: Translation please!

GP: Un mexicano en (name of city in which performance is taking place) es como un turco en Alemania, o como un gitano en España.

RS: Translation please!

GP: Güera-moment, güera! . . .

RS: Translation please!

GP: Me cago en el governador Pito Wilson y en su política xenofóbica de mierda . . .

RS: Translation please!

GP says something in tongues.

RS: Translation please!

GP/DIDACTIC:

Now, let's move to the next stage. Spanish lesson for advanced Spanish speakers. Repeat after me: Los norteamericanos que no aprendieron a hablar español sufrieron una marginación total. No podían encontrar trabajo y en las escuelas multirraciales se les consideraba retrasados mentales. Aquí con nosotros en el estudio #4 de TV Aztlán, tenemos a varios ejemplos de . . .

BLACKOUT.

PROPHECY #V: THE OFFICIAL TRANSCULTURE

GP puts on a mariachi hat and jacket, grabs a machete, and walks towards a hanging chicken. RS puts on a "Gómez-Peña" mask.

MUSIC: "TECOLOTITO" BY ZAZIL

GP pulls a pulsating rubber heart from his crotch and drinks blood from it. Then he dances "El Jarabe Tapatío" drunkenly while trying to stab the chicken. He misses over and over, and ends up falling down.

RS/COMPUTERIZED VOICE:

The Federation of U.S. Republics' fragile sense of self is sustained by a government-sanctioned transnational media culture that is broadcast via Reali-TV, Empty-V, radiorama, and telefax. Its mission is to transmit an idealized and apolitical version of who we are, but unfortunately, it must contend with rebels who operate pirate radio and TV stations throughout the borderless and still nameless continent.

Still, F.U.S.R.'s experience in overthrowing revolutionary groups has made it clear that the best way to contain rebellion is to offer an easier alternative. That's why they're undertaking the current campaign of the amigoization of the North, better known as Operation Jalapeño Fever. This multicultural consumer training project promotes sexy and inoffensive Latino products that range from taco capsules and chili spray to inflatable Fridas and holographic naked mariachis. The "jalapeño fever" helps to diffuse the sense of despair and the frantic search for spirituality found in today's society.

These efforts mark a drastic change from the early days of the New World Order, when democratically elected fascists like Belse-Bush and Mamargaret Thatcher practiced panic politics via TV in order to maintain a generalized state of fear. Do you remember the "War on Drugs," the "AIDS crisis," the "Invasion of Panama," and the "Baghdad Genocide" — the four most successful mini-series produced by the White House? Well, things have really changed.

GP stops dancing and begins to perform hara-kiri in slow motion. Lights off him.

RS: The CIA joined forces with the DEA, and moved to Hollywood to create a movie studio that specializes in producing and distributing multicultural utopias. Free Trade Art can now be purchased by mail order. We can travel arcross the entire continent in a weekend by visiting an Expo. Hybrid pop culture airs during prime time on the main channels of Empty-V. The hit program "Pura Bi-Cultura" reaches 500 million homes in 20,000 cities throughout the New World Border. Fusion rock bands that used to be underground now play their punkarachi, discolmeca, and rap-guanco at NAFTA functions. Transcontinental Radiorama features audio-graffiti art, epic rap poetry, and ethno-muzak, twenty-four hours a day. You'll never get bored, even if you want to.

Are you bored? Why? Too many ideas? Not enough action onstage? Not enough action in your life? Not enough salsa picante on your genitalia? Are you lost in the immediate future? ¡Culero!

SOUNDBED: TAPED EXCERPT OF "NORTE/SUR" *(RADIO PERFORMANCE BY COCO FUSCO & GP)*

GP: *(mouths tape excerpt)* America is no longer the continent you imagine. . . . Audio-graffiti, FM, buscando un nuevo lenguaje para expresar sus temores y deseos interculturales . . .

BLACKOUT.

PROPHECY #VI: THE BARRIOS OF RESISTANCE

GP puts on holographic glasses and pachuco hat.

RS/SATANIC VOICE:

Good evening America . . . Good morning Europe. In reaction to this official transculture, a grassroots octopus with a million tentacles has emerged from below, and hundreds of small pockets of resistance appear everywhere. Together they constitute an invisible artistic continent within the New World Border called Arteamérica Sociedad Anónima. Tape rolling . . .

MUSIC: BRAZILIAN PUNK

GP/LUNATIC, NASAL VOICE:

In the barrios of resistance — contemporary versions of the old kilombos — every block has a secret community center. There, the runaway youths called Robo-Raza II or "floating greasers" publish anarchist laser-xerox magazines, edit experimental home videos on police brutality (yes, police brutality still exists) and broadcast pirate radio interventions like this one over the most popular programs of the official Radio Nuevo Orden.

These clandestine centers are constantly raided, but Robo-Raza II just moves the action to the garage next door. Those who get white-listed can no longer get jobs in the "Mall of Oblivion." And those who get caught en fragante are sent to rehabilitation clinics where they are subjected to instant socialization through em-pedagogic videos (from the Spanish verb *empedar,* meaning to force someone to drink, and the Mayan noun *agogic,* o sea, a man without a self, like many of you).

MUSIC STOPS ABRUPTLY.

RS: Cut! Cut! No cute theatrical tricks, Azteca, just be yourself.

GP: What do you mean? I am being myself!

RS: Stop performing! Get off the fuckin' script!!

GP: Listen Beto Brecht. This section never worked. We haven't even rehearsed it for months, man . . .

RS: Get off the pinche script!!

GP: Okay. . . . This is the last time you put me in the spotlight like this. What do you want me to talk about?

RS: The art world. You are an expert, ¿que no? And it better be funny. These poor people are tired of your density.

GP/NORMAL VOICE:

Okay. . . . Since the art market collapsed, artists are no longer needed as image-makers. Most of them have traded making art for more useful metiers. They have become borderólogos, experts on border-crossing, media pirates, and cross-cultural diplomats. In fact, many of them collaborate in secret with Robo-Raza II.

Due to a counter-intelligence program implemented by former dictator Belse-Bush that involved state censorship of the arts and funding cutbacks, the "alternative space" network and the Chicano community centers have also collapsed.

In the absence of "alternative spaces," most successful performeadores (from the Spanglish *performear*, to piss on your audience) now appear mano a mano with Tex-Mex rockers at extravaganzas staged in abandoned wrestling auditoriums and bullfight arenas like this one. Since Reali-TV doesn't cover these events, we can say that technically they don't exist.

The only thing left from the old "alternative culture" is a leftist porno channel called Pubic Access TV. It specializes in pornostalgic marxist soap operas. Unfortunately, since most people have been desexualized and depoliticized, only .000001 percent of the population watches Pubic Access TV. In this sense, they are a real alternative venue. Have the real TV cameras arrived? *(screaming)* Where the fuck are the TV cameras? *(dramatic pause for approximately ten seconds)*

Censorship has become the main subject of *(he subvocalizes to make it appear as if someone is turning the volume off and on)* . . . 's nothing you can do about it. Even the artists ourselves have . . . fear is the sign of . . . representing a true cross-section of our communities are . . . el idioma español ha sido el principal ob . . .

RS/FORCEFUL:

Speak güey! . . . Speak coño!. . . Say what you want chingao! . . . Get a fuckin' job!

GP can't speak, experiences pain, and begins to cry in frustration.

BLACKOUT.

PROPHECY #VII: THE NEW PAGANISM

Lights on GP & RS. GP does a meditational "om" chant, then makes the "mocos" sign [Mexican hand signal that means "fuck you"] to the audience.

RS/FAKE SINCERITY:

Please stand up, hold hands, and feel the wisdom of the maestro in your genital chakras. Breathe in, breathe out. . . .

GP/CHANTING:

Hare Krishna, Krishnahuatl, hare nalga, hairy nalga . . . *(repeats three times)*

MUSIC: MEXICAN NEW AGE

GP/MEXICAN WRESTLING REFEREE VOICE:

As Protestantism and Catholicism collapse due to their inability to adapt to the Big Change, we witness a revival of pagan religions. New hybrid deities are being adored by the confused masses. *(he grabs a wooden snake and begins to tame it) Tezcatlipunk,* Mexican god of urban wrath is becoming very popular in both Aztlán and Tesmogtitlán. *Funkahuatl,* the Aztec divinity of funk, has been crowned as the Holy Patron of Califas. Aging pop star Madonna has reincarnated as Saint Frida Kahlo. She roams around the nasty streets of Mexa York in search of people who suffer from identity blisters and heals them. *Chichicolgatzin,* the Guru-esa of strippers, is the spiritual avatar of a New Age sect from Colorado. *Krishnahuatl,* the Aztec god of karma, is revered across the entire Federation of U.S. Republics, where thousands of high-tech ashrams infested by world-beat gringostanis and gringofarians provide the "ten steps to clarity" for a modest amount.

A techno-shrine to Juan Soldado, Holy Patron of border-crossers and migrant workers, now stands on what used to be the San Ysidro border checkpoint. With multi-image projections and twenty-five video monitors, the old border saint reminds people of what was once a common, yet dangerous experience.

GP & RS: *(in syncopated rhythm)* The crossing from the Third to the First World; from the past to the future, remember? El cruce, el bordo, el abísmo, el sismo, la migra, the spiderweb, the TV cameras, my old performances, your oldest prejudices, the original migration, your great mojado grandparents. Remember?

BLACKOUT.

PROPHECY #VIII: CULTI-MULTURAL ART

GP squats under chicken #4, chanting in tongues. He puts on a wrestling mask and boxing gloves and prays to the chicken. RS wears a cardboard "Indian" mask.

SOUNDBED: EXCERPT FROM "NORTE/SUR"

RS & GP/SUBVOCALIZING WITH TAPE EXCERPT:

Yaqui, Seri, Guaycura, Diegueño, Barona, Seminole, Coman-chero, Tuscarora, romantic dots on tourist maps, romantic words in empty ears, cambio de canal.

LATIN MUZAK BEGINS.

RS rings a bell. GP stands up and boxes with hanging chicken while repeating compulsively, "I'm beating the Mexican out of myself."

RS/COMPUTERIZED VOICE:

Art about identity is now a dignified form of nostalgia. Nearly every important city in F.U.S.R. has a Museum of Culti-multural Art. They all feature classic shows from the '80s and before as a reminder of what culture used to be before gringostroika destroyed all traditional borders and categories.

Among the most popular traveling exhibits are, "One Thousand Ex-minority Artists," "The Best of Chicano Fundamentalist Painting (1968–1992)," "Triple Oppressions: Bi, Mexican, and Handicapped," and of course, the new show at the San Diego Maquiladora Museum of Contrived Art entitled "Chic-anglo Art on the Borderline."

Just last month, a very controversial show opened at the Museum of Lost Identity in Los Angeles. Entitled "Clepto-Mexican Artists of the Early '90s," it includes thirty major Anglo-American painters whose iconography mysteriously resembles that of their Mexican contemporaries.

Bell rings. GP stops boxing and freezes, then lights off him.

RS: Fem-arte, a collective of Frida-worshiping feminists, picketed the show's opening to protest the lack of Anglo women included in the clepto-Mexican panorama. They all wore body casts and pierced their chests to dramatize their sense of victimization.

GP takes off wrestler mask, puts on "Caucasian" mask, and sits in his chair. Lights on him. RS takes off his mask and puts on a blond wig.

GP/FRENCH ACCENT:

Every now and then, these outdated museums present token Eurocentric shows with insensitive titles such as "The Europassé Vanguard," "Neo-Geo: A Post-Industrial Folk Art," "Land and Body Art: Early Gringo Tribalism," "Minimalist Sculpture: Protestant Art in an Agnostic Society," and "The Young German Expressionists: An Endangered Species," but these kind of shows are poorly attended, and don't seem to perform any real community function other than fulfilling the extravagant whims of iconoclastic curators.

Two post-Chicano antropolocos (Richie Lou and Bobby Sánchez) are currently organizing a blackbuster exhibit entitled "Ex-plendors: 3,000 Years of White Art," but they are facing tremendous opposition. Minority artists are faulting them for ghettoization and tokenism.

RS barks during next paragraph.

GP/NEUROTIC GRINGO ACCENT:

No one can escape this wave of reverse racism. A critic from the minority paper the *New York Times* just accused Super-Pocho and I of "latinocentrism" for not having included waspbacks in this show, but the fact is that . . . their work is simply not good enough! Have you had similar experiences?

(misspelled Spanish) Yo no entenderr un carrayo de porqui la mayorría dominanti de color nagro, café or amarrilo tenemos que . . . Shit!

NORMAL VOICE:

Cut! Cut!! I don't like this take. It's racist! Let's do it again! Cameras one and two rolling . . . down . . . your . . . psyche. Hasta el fondo y el cansancio.

BLACKOUT.

RS takes off wig and jacket and walks toward center stage.

PROPHECY #IX: THE MAFIAS

GP puts on bandana and dark glasses and lights a joint. During next text, RS turns into a "gang member" and begins to "desecrate" a chicken. He covers his T-shirt with chicken blood.

RS/TOURIST GUIDE VOICE:

Latinophobe . . . polyglophobe . . . ecoracist . . . criptonationalist . . . technopuritan . . . define yourself . . . define yourself . . . define yourself . . .

GP/SATANIC VOICE:

Fear of uncertainty generates sectarianism, therefore mafias are forming everywhere. Their members used to be part of the "cultural elite" during the Belse-Bush years. Though extremely different from one another, these mafias share one objective: to cling to the past in order to experience an optical illusion of continuity and order. The following are some examples. Note that they still utilize the old nomenclature to name themselves:

SOUNDBED: ANIMAL SOUNDS (CATS, DOGS, COWS, PIGS, ROOSTERS, AND SHEEP)

RS/DIDACTIC:

Please raise your hands as your group is being mentioned.

GP/CONTINUES WHILE RS DEFINES THE GROUPS:

The elite of the artists of color of my generation formed a group called TGAC (**Thin & Gorgeous Artists of Color**). They make high-tech post–colonial art and organize symposiums with other members of TGAC from Europe. Their criteria for inclusion are very strict. They don't let me in because my Mexican't mustache and my hipiteca pony-tail reveal an obvious lack of sophistication. **Are there any members of TGAC here?**

Both WWEO (**White Women Experts of Otherness**) and MGW (**Multicultural Gabachos from Wyoming**) claim they are solely responsible for the liberation of the veterans of LVIR (**Leading Victims of Institutionalized Racism**). This group was formed by the elite members of the various ex-minority groups who won victim competitions at the Multicultural Olympics of 1992.

The violent members of SWGAA (**Straight White Guys Are Alright**) couldn't bear the Big Change anymore and went underground. Some people speculate that they asked for political asylum in Germany and England, but to their surprise, they found even more people of color over there.

The members of CRF (**Chicken Rights Falange**) a radical wing of the deceased Animal Rights Coallision of the early '90s, roam around theaters and natural history museums, picketing events like this one. **Would you please raise your hands?**

Composed of ex-Sandinista poets in exile, the Berkeley-based LCS (**La Cosa Sandinostra**) survives by selling political kitsch and meditational revolutionary CDs. Ojo: We must not mistake this mafia with Los Sandalistas, which literally means "**those bearded gringos with plastic Indian shoes.**"

The members of BAL (**Born Again Latinos**) defend a distinct "Latinou" identity at a time when essentialism has been outlawed by the state, and they are very militant about it. They are suspected of the recent bombings of several museums of culti-multural art.

The secret brotherhood of CHAELA (Chicano Aristocracy from East LA), believe that Adam and Eve were the first pochos and that Chicanos are the chosen race. Their leader, named Vatoman, is on death row for conspiracy to overthrow the New World Border.

Located in the Independent Republic of Harlem, RAN (the Real African Nation) claims that the entire African continent sold out, and it is no longer African enough. This organization must not be confused with the other RAN (the Real Aztec Nation) which is a group of UCLA anthropologists who swear they have the one and only secret to the Aztec way of life: the untranslatable "tajoditzin." O mejor dicho, mejor me callo. I turn off my inner radio.

GP grabs a machete, walks toward the hanging chicken, grabs its head, and decapitates it while saying:
Chick . . . chick . . . en . . . oh . . . no . . . Chicano . . . Power
(he raises his right fist)

BLACKOUT.

FINALE

The performers grab two chairs and sit on the edge of the stage, with brown bags covering their faces. Slowly all house lights come up.

PRERECORDED VOICE:
The performance is finally over. Now, would anyone like to spend the night with a sexy, AIDS-free, Third World performance artist for only twenty-five pesos? Free Trade Sex, the ultimate border experience. Please, feel free to walk on stage and touch them, lick them, smell them, but don't go too far unless you are willing to pay the piper. The Mexican male on the right weighs seventy-five kilos and loves German cinema. Although still undocumented, he has been

Photo by Dirk Bakker

blessed by a MacArthur Genie Award. The younger Chicano on the left plays soccer with Central American refugees, speaks French, and makes a mean enchilada. They are not trained actors, but they have great imagination and charisma. Go for it. Don't be culeros.

SILENCE.

Loud Mexican rock 'n' roll suddenly breaks the dramatic tension. The audience begins to applaud. Some people walk onstage and touch the performers. Eventually, GP & RS stand up and take the bags off their heads.

— THE END —

I JUST DON'T KNOW WHAT TO THINK OF YOUR COUNTRY

Dear M,
I still don't know what to think of your country
it gave me the chanza to be listened to and respected
for my particular kind of madness — type B —
but it also destroyed my favorite uncles
& half of my liver
temporarily mutilated my political self
turned my sister Diana into a moonie
and my nephew Cristóbal into a beach zombie
this marvelous and sinister country
has offered me my best friends
& most dangerous enemies
all the prizes an artist could desire
& all the horrors a Mexican might face
— 9 prizes and 8 police busts, to be precise —
coma,
dearísima M,
this nameless country of yours
deleted my original identity
and replaced it with a brand-new hybrid self:
el homo fronterizus (1955–?)
I just don't know what to think of your country
for the moment
I'm taking a trip back to Mexico
bruja, my tongue and muscles need some serious rest

Signed: el resident alien
          in search of a new residence
          ¡la tuya!

Real-life Border Thriller

REAL-LIFE BORDER THRILLER

I AM THE PROUD FATHER OF A FOUR-YEAR-OLD BOY, GUILLERMO Emiliano Gómez-Hicks, who happens to be half-Mexican, perfectly bilingual, and blond. I call him "el güero de Aztlán." He has asked me several times, "Papa, how come you are brown and I am pink?" Last month, he finally learned what that means.

On April 8, 1993, I went to San Diego for my regular monthly visit with my son, but this time my visit turned into a cross-cultural nightmare. My son, my ex-wife, and I were having lunch at Chez Odette in Hillcrest, a fashionable neighborhood that prides itself on being an island of tolerance and diversity amidst the city's ultraconservatism. We talked about the plans for my weekend visit with Guillermito. I vaguely remember two blond women staring at us intently from another table.

We left the café, and I hailed a Yellow Cab. My ex-wife opened the trunk of her car and handed me my son's little suitcases. Guillermo Jr. and I got into the cab and went to my friend, filmmaker Isaac Artenstein's house in Coronado, where we were going to spend the night. In the cab, we chatted in Spanish about going to Los Angeles to visit some friends.

After arriving in Coronado, we decided to go out for a walk in the park. At around 2 P.M. we were strolling back to the house when suddenly we were stopped by a Coronado policeman. The officer looked very nervous. He asked if I had been at a café on Fifth Avenue at around noon. I answered affirmatively. He asked if I had taken a Yellow Cab to Adela Lane in Coronado. I said yes, again. He then said into his radio: "I have the suspect."

He was talking to the San Diego police, telling them exactly where we were. I asked him for an explanation. He said he was "just cooperating with the San Diego police," and that all he knew was "that it had something to do with a kidnapping." I understood right away that I was being accused of kidnapping my own child.

For forty-five minutes, my son and I were held by the Coronado policeman, waiting for his San Diego colleagues to arrive. I was furious and completely devastated. I held Guillermito's hand tightly. I thought to myself, if the police try to take my son away from me, I'll fight back with all my strength. Guillermito kept asking me, "How come we can't go? What's happening, Papa?" And I answered, "It's just a movie, don't worry."

I was able to control my feelings, and politely asked the police officer to let me identify myself. He agreed. Very carefully, I pulled out my wallet and showed him my press card, an integral part of my "Mexican survival kit" in the United States. The cop turned purple. "Are you a journalist?" he inquired. "Yes," I answered, "and you and your colleagues had better give me a detailed explanation of what is happening, because I'm going to write about it!" He realized the mistake he'd made, and tried to compensate in a clumsy manner by showing my son the technological wonders of his patrol car. Guillermito was unimpressed and scared. He hugged my leg.

Finally, a sweaty and agitated San Diego policeman, officer Robert Roche arrived, ready for some action. Luckily, the Coronado cop took him aside and spoke to him in private, probably to warn him about the fact that he'd seen my press card. Officer Roche's attitude changed dramatically. I asked him to explain why I was suspected of kidnapping my own son. He told me the following story:

At 12:10 P.M., the police received a 911 call from a woman who claimed that a Latino man with a mustache and a ponytail and "a woman who also looked suspicious" were sitting at a café with an Anglo boy "who didn't look like he belonged to them." She said that the boy "was clearly being held against his will." She emphasized the fact that I was speaking to my son in Spanish and, despite the fact that she didn't speak or understand Spanish herself, concluded that I "was trying to bribe the child with presents" and "talking about taking him to Mexico." As we left the café, the woman and a friend of hers followed us and watched us take my son's suitcases out of his mother's car and get into the cab. They called the police again and told them that I "had forced the kid into the taxi." They provided the police with the license-plate numbers of both the taxi and my ex-wife's car.

The police proceeded to call the Yellow Cab company and obtained the driver's radio number. They tried to contact him, but apparently the radio was disconnected. The police concluded from this that I had not only abducted my blond son, but "that [I] was probably holding the taxi driver hostage with a weapon and that [we] were probably heading toward the border."

According to Roche, the officer in charge of directing this B-movie was Sergeant Mike Gibbs, from the SDPD's Western Division. They quickly dispatched several helicopters and alerted units citywide to comb the streets in search of an armed kidnapper. They even sent units to the international line and alerted the border patrol.

I couldn't believe my ears. It sounded like a comedic thriller co-directed by Fassbinder and Cheech Marin. I tried not to show any outrage, so as to give officer Roche the confidence to continue telling me his version of the story:

After the cab dropped my son and me at my friend's house, the police finally succeeded in contacting the driver, who told them that while the suspect didn't hold him up, "he did speak in Spanish to the kid." Led to the residence by the cab driver, four policemen surrounded the house with their guns drawn. Three of them broke into the empty house at gunpoint — without a search warrant — and went through every room.

"In cases like this one, a search warrant is not necessary," officer Roche explained. "We feared that a child's life was in danger." My son and I were extremely lucky. Apparently, the police arrived at the house just a few minutes after we had left. Knowing the San Diego Police Department's track record, had we been there, the possibility of a tragic outcome would have been very real.

I asked Roche what they found inside the house. He told me that they saw photographs and "some letters in Spanish, which [they] couldn't read." Again, the Spanish language was a major factor in the crescendo of my process of criminalization.

Once they were sure the place was empty, they brought the cab driver into the kitchen where my friends have a bulletin board with family photos. He mistook film producer Jude Eberhard for my ex-wife, San Diego State University professor Emily Hicks.

The plot was becoming increasingly outrageous and racist. At one point, Roche noted that the "cab driver was stupid," in spite of the fact that he was Anglo, "'cause, you know, Anglos tend to be much more intelligent . . ." He paused. The end of the sentence was more than implied.

At this point I realized that I needed a witness. I asked officer Roche to please take my son and me to my friends' home, in the hope that one of them was already back from work. The house had been locked by the police, and I didn't have a key. I asked Roche to please drive us to Isaac and Jude's café, the popular Cafe Cinema at the corner of Front Street and Cedar, and to explain to them what had just happened.

On our way, I asked him if there had been any recent reports of missing children that encouraged the police to believe the women who phoned from the café. He said no. Then I asked him to explain to me how could there be a kidnapping without a report of a missing child. He replied that "many foreigners kidnap kids and take them across the border. Once you cross that border, you never know." He reminded me of "that famous case of this Egyptian or Iranian guy who kidnapped his son from his American ex-wife and took him to the Middle East." I told him I didn't see any connection to my case and suggested to him that perhaps racism had played an important role in the misunderstanding. Roche became visibly upset. He insisted that there had been no racial bias whatsoever and that I should be grateful because "it could have been a true kidnapping. I mean, think for a second, what if it had been true?" This, I call postmodern logic.

Once at Cafe Cinema, officer Roche repeated his version of the story to Jude. When my friend asked if they had a search warrant, he said once again that it wasn't necessary and that "if the door had been locked, we could have legally broken it."

I phoned my ex-wife and told her to call the police department immediately to identify herself as the mother of the never-abducted child, and the owner of the other "suspicious" vehicle. An officer with a Spanish surname told her verbatim: "Don't worry, you have already been taken out of the computer. And by the way, you should be grateful. This incident proves how quickly the San Diego police can act."

When interrogated about the motivations of the manhunt by *Los Angeles Times* journalist Sebastian Rotella, San Diego police spokesman Bill Robinson denied any ethnic bias in the police actions, citing instead a recent case of the abduction of two kids who were found dead in the San Diego area as the primary motivation for their overreaction. What he didn't tell the *Times* was that in all recent kidnappings, the criminals have been Anglo. Despite the fact that officer Roche told me twice that several helicopters had been dispatched, the police spokesman down-played the scale of the manhunt and told the *L.A. Times* that only one helicopter had been involved in the operation.

Rotella was also told that local television reporters had heard about the manhunt while it was taking place, and that they were demanding more details from the police to complete the story for the evening news. Perhaps if my son and I hadn't been detained quickly and allowed to clarify the dangerous misunderstanding, the evening news would have included a sensational case of the abduction of an Anglo child by an armed Mexican.

The following weeks were very stressful for my son, for my friends, and for me. My mind couldn't stop revising all the possible scenarios. If the police suspected, as Roche had told me, that I was armed, what would have happened if my son, or I, or anyone else had been in the house when they broke in? How would I have reacted if suddenly my son and I were surrounded by three agitated cops pointing their guns at us? What if, possessed by fear, we had tried to hide or run? And what would have happened if we didn't come back to the house until late at night? By then, the entire city would have been in a state of hysteria and the police reaction could have been far more extreme. What if, like thousands of Mexicans in San Diego, I didn't speak English or didn't have a press card with me?

When I finally came out of my shock, I realized that what had just happened to my son and me wasn't that strange or unusual. Every day, thousands of "suspicious-looking" Latinos in the United States are victims of police harassment, civilian vigilantism, racial paranoia, and cultural misunderstanding. "Mistaken identity" is nothing but a euphemism for racism. Latinos and other people of color are regularly "mistaken" for "illegal aliens," gang members, drug dealers, and rapists, and often these "mistakes" lead to far more extreme resolutions such as incarceration, beatings by patriotic civilians or policemen, and deportations.

Since "the incident" was publicized in the media, dozens of people of color have contacted me to tell me similar stories. A Mexican man in San Diego was publicly humiliated by a mob during the Persian Gulf crisis; they though he was Iraqi. An African American man was chased by his girlfriend's concerned neighbors after he entered her building; "He looked like a rapist," they told her. A young Colombian man went to the San Francisco police department to obtain a record for immigration purposes; he was detained and interrogated for six hours because he looked like someone they were after. Perhaps the only difference in my case is that I had the capacity to respond, the connections to defend myself, and that handy press card.

I am deeply hurt. Experiences like this one cannot be forgotten that easily. I especially blame the two racist civilian vigilantes who decided that a Latino man holding a blond kid's hand had to be a criminal. If I had been blond and my kid dark, the assumption would have been quite different: "Look, how cute. He probably adopted the child." If I had been a Latina, perhaps the assumption would have been, "She's probably the nanny or the baby-sitter." But the deadly combination is a dark-skinned man with a blond child — the representations of evil and innocence in the American mythos.

And I blame the city of San Diego for breeding anti-Mexican sentiment and paranoia. A great majority of Anglo San Diegans live in constant fear of their enigmatic neighbors. For them, a Mexican walking down the wrong street, or a group of Mexicans speaking in Spanish at a public place are signs of imminent danger. I also blame the arrogant San Diego police for jeopardizing my son's life and the life of whoever could have been in the house when they broke in on the basis of pure speculation. A month has passed, and the police still haven't apologized for what they did.

Guillermito has learned a very sad lesson. His teacher told my ex-wife that since "the incident," he has been omitting his father's last name when signing his drawings. He is also falling asleep wherever he goes. His tender mind is unable to understand exactly what happened and why. All he knows is that to go out with Daddy can be a dangerous experience.

I strongly believe in the moral power of an apology to partially restore our damaged dignity. I won't stop writing, talking, and lecturing about "the incident" until the San Diego police and the two women who originally invented this surreal plot decide to publicly apologize to us, in both English and Spanish. A bilingual public apology will also remind the thousands of civilian vigilantes, amateur Charles Bronsons, Texas Rangers wannabes, and racist cops roaming around the city that the next time they see a "suspicious-looking" Latino, he might be able to defend himself intelligently.

Living diorama from "The Museum of Frozen Identity." The accompanying museum label reads: "El Mexterminator (alias Mad-Mex). Characteristics: undocumented; drug user; extremely violent; hyper-sexual; highly politicized; speaks in Spanglish; practices witchcraft, karate, and performance. He is indestructible. Political Project: To reclaim Aztlán, *by any means.*" Museo de la Ciudad de México, 1996. Photo by Monica Naranjo

* This performance character was designed collectively by over 5,000 Internet users.

I COULD ONLY FIGHT BACK IN MY POETRY

Performed live as "El Quebradito," a flamboyant vaquero from northern Mexico, dressed in a fake zebra-skin tuxedo. He looks tired and crestfallen, and his voice is raspy. Soundbed: Music by guitar maestro Antonio Bribiesca plays on a ghetto blaster; the irritating voice of an evangelist preacher can be heard in the distance.

it was the spring of '87 in the city of Arlington
I tried to explain to you in my very broken English
that Texas had once been a Mexican ranch
& that truth was not a "gringo-bashing ideology"
but you had seen too many Stallone films
& felt obliged to let me have it, ¿que no?
so you tried to beat the Meskin out of me
of course, since you were a foot taller & 85 lbs.
    heavier
& not that skilled in cross-cultural diplomacy
I could only fight back in my poetry
in fact, I'm fighting back right now
you claimed you hated my accent & my arrogance
but the real reason you despised me
was that your wife was just about to leave you
& hit the road to sexy Mexico
to escape the Texan nightmare, your inflexible arms,
your smelly feet & psychotic eyes
so Mexico became the source of all your fears
the red-light district where gringos are poisoned by
    midget whores
the mountain of trash where kids with typhoid make
    holes to sleep in

the bus that keeps breaking down on your way to
  some generic jungle
the gentle mariachi who touched your wife like you
  never did
you saw all these images in my eyes before you broke
  my ribs
& I could only fight back in my poetry

P.S. #1 I don't harbor any resentments but I sure
   hope one of these days you learn to read &
   write

P.S. #2 See, I told you culero, I win most fights in
   the streets of my poetry

P.S. #3 I heard you joined the militia movement
   last month. . . . I must say that you are
   consistent in misplacing your anger, man

THE PSYCHO IN THE LOBBY OF THE THEATER

A psychotic-looking man in a wrinkled suit has been waiting for me in the lobby since 10 A.M. He's got a mysterious Samsonite briefcase on his lap. It's spooky! I always come across these locos, and I've learned that the best way to deal with them is through poetic confrontation. So, I take a deep breath and approach him:

are you waiting for someone, sir?
he looks at me in silence
waiting
merely waiting, eh?
waiting for what, exactly?
he doesn't answer me
waiting for the economy to improve?
silence
waiting for your children to leave home
and for all the immigrants to leave "your" country?
waiting for God to come back from India
or speak to you on Cable TV?
waiting for the next hysterical talk show
to address your most sincere concerns?
he doesn't answer & I become increasingly exasperated
waiting for the next best-seller
on how to improve the quality of your loneliness?
it's lonely out there, ¿que no?
silence
come on, you gotta answer me
what are you fuckin' waiting for?!
waiting for the next cheap vacation to Mazatlán?

for more vouchers & coupons?
for a random bullet, perhaps?
waiting, insomniac in your underwear,
to hear from your drinking buddies, aquellos,
while you pick another fight with your desperate
        wife?
(*jadeante/encabronado*) come on, answer me!!
incommensurable silence
no mister,
it's pointless to keep waiting
this is the year of the barking dog . . .
& I'm afraid your fears are . . . much bigger than
        your wishes
he stands up, his eyes wide-open, like a fish
I shake his hand
you might be wondering who the hell I am?
the man is scared and still unable to reply
I am your worst fear, caballero
an unpredictable Mexican with a huge mustache
3 chips on his shoulder
& extra-hot sauce on his cobra tongue
I begin to bark
he finally breaks his silence:
"It's a pleasure to meet you. My name is Mario
        López.
I came to fix the xerox machine."

I go back to rehearsal feeling utterly embarrassed. That night I tell
the story to my audience. They crack up. The hapless victim of my poetic
chamber of tortures, Mr. López himself is sitting right in the front row.
    I feel like killing myself.
    I truly do.

WADSWORTH   McBEE

The Border Patrol's
"smallest" catch
EL PASO TEXAS ABOUT 1929

Photo courtesy of *The Broken Line* archives

THE '90s CULTURE OF XENOPHOBIA: Beyond the Tortilla Curtain

Americans never remember; Mexicans never forget.
— popular Mexican saying

THE CAPITAL OF THE AMERICAN CRISIS

From 1978 to 1991, I lived and worked in and among the cities of Tijuana, San Diego, and Los Angeles. Like hundreds of thousands of Mexicans living at the border, I was a binational commuter. I crossed that dangerous border regularly, by plane, by car, and on foot. The border became my home, my base of operations, and my laboratory for social and artistic experimentation. My art, my dreams, my family and friends, and my psyche were literally and conceptually divided by the border. But the border was not a straight line; it was more like a Möbius strip. No matter where I was, I was always on "the other side," feeling ruptured and incomplete, ever longing for my other selves, my other home and tribe.

Thanks to my Chicano colleagues and border accomplices, I learned to perceive California as an extension of Mexico; and the city of Los Angeles as the northernmost barrio of Mexico City. And despite many Californians' denial of their state's Mexican past and their bittersweet relationship with contemporary Mexicans, I never quite felt like an immigrant. As a mestizo with a thick accent and an even thicker mustache, I knew I wasn't exactly welcome, but I also knew that millions of Latinos, "legal" and "illegal," Mexican or not, shared that border experience with me.

Then in 1991, I moved to New York City, and my umbilical cord was finally snapped. For the first time in my life, I felt like a true immigrant. From my Brooklyn apartment, Mexico and Chicanolandia seemed a million light years away. (The republic of Mexa York was still a project yet to be realized.)

I decided to return to Southern Califas in 1993. Since the riots, Los Angeles had become the epicenter of America's social, racial, and cultural crisis. It was, unwillingly, the capital of a growing Third World within the shrinking First World. I wanted to be both a witness and a chronicler of this wonderful madness.

I found a city at war with itself; a city gravely punished by natural and social forces; a city whose experience is a concentrated version of the crises confronting the entire country. Its political structures are dysfunctional and its economy is in shambles; cutbacks in the defense budget have resulted in increased unemployment; and racial tensions are the focus of daily news reports. Crime rates and poverty levels can be compared with those of any Third World city. All this coincides with an unprecedented crisis of national identity: post–Cold War America is having a very hard time shedding its imperial nostalgia, embracing its multiracial soul, and accepting its new status as the first "developed" country to become a member of the Third World.

Perhaps what scared me most was to realize who was being blamed for all the turmoil. The Mexican/Latino immigrant community was the scapegoat, singled out by politicians (both Republicans and Democrats), fanatic citizen groups like SOS [Save Our State], and by sectors of the mainstream media as the main cause of California's social ills. The racist Proposition 187, which denies nonemergency medical services and education to "illegal aliens," passed with 60 percent of the vote on November 8, 1994, turning every doctor, nurse, pharmacist, policeman, schoolteacher and "concerned citizen" into a de facto border patrolman. Furthermore, the very same people who supported Prop. 187 (which is now being challenged in the courts) also opposed women's and gay rights, affirmative action, bilingual education, freedom of speech, and the existence of the National Endowment for the Arts and the Corporation for Public Broadcasting. Why? What does this all mean? What are we all losing?

> *You are the posse and 187 is the rope.*
> — Orange County rightwinger

GODZILLA WITH A MARIACHI HAT

Despite the fact that the United States has been a nation of immigrants and border crossers ever since its violent foundation, nativism has periodically reared its head. American identity has historically depended on opposing an "other," be it cultural, racial, or ideological. Americans need enemies against whom to define their personal and national boundaries. From the original indigenous inhabitants of this continent to the former Soviets, an evil "other" has always been stalking and ready to strike.

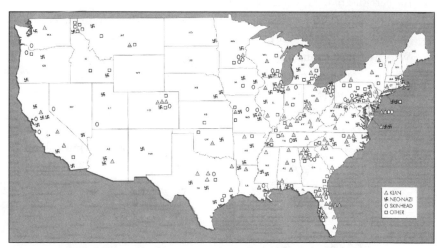

Documented hate groups in the United States in 1994.
From the *Klanwatch Intelligence Report,* March 1995

65

Now, it is the "illegal aliens" who are to take the blame for everything that American citizens and their incompetent politicians have been unable (or unwilling) to solve. Undocumented immigrants are being stripped of their humanity and individuality, becoming blank screens for the projection of Americans' fear, anxiety, and rage. In California and other southwestern states, this threatening otherness comes in a huge package that includes Mexicans, Latinos (including U.S.-born Latinos), Mexican-looking people (whatever this means), Mexican and Chicano culture, and the Spanish language. This horrible menace is here, inside of "our" country, within "our" borders, not only threatening "our" jobs and neighborhoods, but also "our" ideals of justice and order.

Anti-immigration has become a galvanizing force behind the resurgence of a phony form of patriotism. "True" Americans (as opposed to the dark-skinned invaders) perceive themselves as the victims of immigration: "If it wasn't for *them,* everything would be all right." Of all the current arguments against immigration, perhaps the one most often used is that the United States is not as able to absorb immigrants as it was in the past; the Statue of Liberty is exhausted, and she needs a break. What is not stated openly is that she needs a break mainly from immigrants of color; the most "different" ones; those who are less willing or able to assimilate. Sadly, sectors of the Latino and African American communities also subscribe to these bizarre nativist beliefs, forgetting that they themselves are perceived as part of the problem. In the eyes of the xenophobes, any person with visibly different features, skin color, accent, clothes, or social or sexual behavior is an alien.

Illegal aliens are a category of criminal, not a category of ethnic group.
— Proposition 187 advocate Ron Prince

THE BLURRING OF THE BORDER

Fear is always at the core of xenophobia. This fear is particularly disturbing when directed at the most vulnerable victims: migrant workers. They become the "invaders" from the South, the human incarnation of the Mexican fly, subhuman "wetbacks," the "alien" from another (cultural) planet. They are accused of stealing "our jobs," of shrinking "our budget," of taking advantage of the welfare system, of not paying taxes, and of bringing disease, drugs, street violence, foreign thoughts, pagan rites, primitive customs, and alien sounds. Their indigenous features and rough clothes conjure images of an unpleasant pre-European American past, and of the mythical lands to the south immersed in poverty and political turmoil, where innocent gringos could be attacked for no apparent reason. Yet, these invaders no longer inhabit the remote past, some banana republic, or a Hollywood film. They actually live down the block, and their children attend the same schools as the Anglo kids.

Nothing is scarier than the blurring of the border between them and us; between the Dantesque South and the prosperous North; between paganism and Christianity. For many Americans, the border has failed to stop chaos and crisis from creeping in (the origin of crisis and chaos is somehow always located outside). Their worst nightmare is finally coming true: The United States is no longer a fictional extension of Europe, or the wholesome suburb imagined by the screenwriter of *Lassie.* It is rapidly becoming a huge border zone, a hybrid society, a mestizo race, and worst of all, this process seems to be irreversible. America shrinks day by day, as the pungent smell of enchiladas fills the air and the volume of quebradita music rises.

Both the anti-immigration activists and the conservative media have utilized extremely charged metaphors to describe this process of

"Mexicanization." It is described as a Christian nightmare ("hell at our doorsteps"); a natural disaster ("the brown wave"); a fatal disease or an incurable virus; a form of demographic rape; a cultural invasion; or the scary beginning of a process of secession or "Quebequization" of the entire Southwest.

Paradoxically, the country allegedly responsible for all of these anxieties is now an intimate business partner of the United States. But NAFTA only regulates the exchange of consumer products; human beings are not part of the deal. Our new economic community advocates open markets and closed borders, and as NAFTA goes into effect, the Tortilla Curtain is being replaced by a metallic wall that resembles the one that "fell" in Berlin.

> *"If you catch 'em [Mexicans], skin 'em and fry 'em yourself.*
> — Harold Ezell, head of SOS and
> Western Regional Commissioner of the INS

THE CONTRADICTIONS OF UTOPIA

Many Americans easily forget that thanks to "illegal" Mexicans hired by other Americans, the food, garment, tourist, and construction industries of California and the rest of the Southwest survive. They forget that the strawberries, apples, grapes, oranges, tomatoes, lettuce, and avocadoes that they eat were harvested, prepared, and served by Mexican hands. And that these very same "illegal" hands clean up after them in restaurants and bars, fix their broken cars, paint and mop their homes, and manicure their gardens. They also forget that their babies and elderly are being cared for by Mexican nannies. The list of underpaid contributions by "illegal aliens" is so long that the lifestyle of many Americans couldn't possibly be sustained without them. Yet the Americans who are against illegal immigration prefer to believe that their cities and neighborhoods are less safe, and that their cultural and educational institutions have lowered their standards since we were allowed in.

What begins as inflammatory rhetoric eventually becomes accepted dictum, justifying racial violence against suspected illegal immigrants. What Operation Gatekeeper, Proposition 187, and SOS have done is to send a very frightening message to society: The governor is behind you; let those "aliens" have it. Since they are here "illegally," they are expendable. Since they have no "legal residency," they lack both human and civil rights. To hurt, attack, or offend a faceless and nameless "criminal" doesn't seem to have any legal or moral implications. Precisely because of their undocumented condition, the "aliens" are not protected if they talk back, or decide to organize politically. If they demonstrate or engage in direct political actions, or if they report a crime to the police, they risk deportation. When the police or the border patrol abuse their human rights, there is nowhere to go for help. They are the easy targets of state violence, economic exploitation, and civilian vigilantism. And quite often, neither the police nor the citizenry can differentiate between an "illegal alien" and a U.S.-born Latino.

SUICIDAL MEASURES AND ENLIGHTENED PROPOSALS

Authoritarian solutions to "the problem" of immigration can only make things worse. Further militarizing the border while dismantling the social, medical, and educational support systems that serve the immigrant population will only worsen social tensions. Denying medical services to undocumented immigrants will result in more disease and more teenage pregnancy. Throwing 300,000 kids out of the schools and into the streets will only contribute to crime and social disintegration. Not only will these proposals backfire, but they will also contribute to a growing nationalism in the Chicano/Latino communities, repoliticizing entire communites that were dormant in the past decade — any community under attack tends to be more defiant.

So, what to do with "the problem" of immigration? First of all, we need to stop characterizing it as a unilateral "problem." Let's be honest: The end of the century appears scary to both Anglos and Latinos; to legal and illegal immigrants. Both sides feel threatened, uprooted, and displaced, to different degrees and for different reasons. We all fear deep inside that there won't be enough jobs, food, air, and housing for everybody. Yet we cannot deny the processes of interdependence that define our contemporary experience as North Americans. In a post-NAFTA/post–Cold War America, the binary models of us/them, North/South, and Third World/First World are no longer useful in understanding our complicated border dynamics, our transnational identities and our multiracial communities.

It is time to face the facts: Anglos won't go back to Europe, and Mexicans and Latinos (legal or illegal) won't go back to Latin America. We are all here to stay. For better or for worse, our destinies and aspirations are in one another's hands. For me, the only solution lies in a paradigm shift: the recognition that we all are the protagonists in the creation of a new cultural topography and a new social order, one in which we all are "others," and we need the other "others" to exist. Hybridity is no longer up for discussion. It is a demographic, racial, social, and cultural fact.

The real tasks ahead of us are to embrace more fluid and tolerant notions of personal and national identity, and to develop models of peaceful coexistence and multilateral cooperation across nationality, race, gender, and religion. To attain this, rather than more border patrols, border walls, and punitive laws, we need more and better information about one another. Culture and education are at the core of the solution. We need to learn each others' languages, histories, art, and cultural traditions. We need to educate our children and teenagers about the dangers of racism and the complexities of living in a multiracial, borderless society — the inevitable society of the next century.

The role that artists and cultural organizations can perform in this paradigm shift is crucial. Artists can function as community brokers, citizen diplomats, ombudsmen, and border translators. And our art spaces can perform the multiple roles of sanctuaries, demilitarized zones, centers for activism against xenophobia, and informal think tanks for intercultural and transnational dialogue. Collaborative projects among artists from different communities and nationalities can send a strong message to the larger society: Yes, we can talk to one another. We can get along, despite our differences, our fear, and our rage.

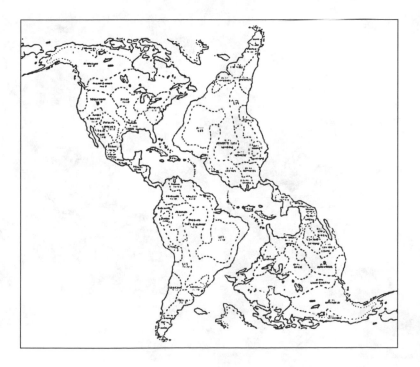

News from Aztlán Liberado

Chicano border patrolmen chasing a group of panicked waspbacks.

NEWS FROM AZTLÁN LIBERADO

Imagine for a moment, a continent turned upside down. . . . You turn on your TV and see a Chicano anchorman, his face covered in pre-Columbian tattoos, looking at you intently. He begins to deliver the news:

Good evening, choliza, robo-raza & white minorities. This weekend has been a particularly intense chapter in the young history of Aztlán liberado. At the top of the news tonight:

35 Mexican citizens have been executed by Anglo gang members.

In an act of random violence, two unemployed corporate executives walked into a luxurious Taco Bell Bistro and fired upon the peaceful fajita-eating customers. Today's headline in the minority paper, the *New York Times* reads: "Blood and guacamole all over the walls; a macabre scene."

The police have surrounded residential East L.A. to block the entrance of angry gringo mobs protesting poor salaries and police brutality.

The governors of Chihuahua, Sonora, and Baja California have issued a formal complaint to the Waspanos in the West Bank who venture illegally into Mexican territory bringing dirt, disease, drugs, prostitution & automatic weapons with them.

Anglo mercenaries — ex-members of the defunct U.S. Army in cahoots with various skinhead tribes — continue to attack several Chicano cities in the Southwest.

The political wing of the Anglo Liberation Front — the former Republican party — has finally gone underground. Sub-comandantes Buchanan & Gingrich are demanding amnesty for all political prisoners, the total restoration of white supremacist TV programming & the immediate reopening of all Protestant temples.

Their communiqué is in response to the upcoming Pacoima Trial, also known as the Raza Tribunal, which begins next week. 117 gringo war criminals will be processed by a select jury of 2,000 homeboys and ex-migrant workers. The defense attorneys are protesting the lack of Anglo representation on the jury.

The most sinister war criminals include Pito Wilson, Harold Ezell (head of narco-citizen group SOS — Ese o Essse), and Darryl Gates, alias "El Puertas." They are accused of rounding up over 10,000 Mexicans and confining them in concentration camps euphemisti-cally called "juvenile halls" and "INS detention centers."

Gates & Wilson are currently being extradited by the Argentine government.

Archbishop Matias has declared all Catholic churches sanctuaries for illegal waspbacks, in defiance of the panic politics of Califas' Governor Molina.

Last week, Molina issued an order to begin deporting "all insubordinate gringos who don't carry the national identity card." She stated at a press conference held at Hotel Fiesta Aztlán *(translation into English)*: "All Mexamericans must stick together in these chaotic times & make sure that the illegal tax-evading waspbacks don't continue to drain our economy and take advantage of our medical, educational, social and cultural institutions." She clarified: "This is not reverse racism, but mere financial pragmatism."

I must say, she's got a point.
After all, 30 million vatos can't all be wrong.

For ABC Televisión Nacional Bilingüe,
this is El Naftazteca servidor
fumigating your post–colonial dreams.

Anglomalan family besieged by Indian bikers.

Zapatista bullfighter on strike in Mexico City's Zócalo, June 1995. Photo by Jesus Avila

CHICANOST: RADIO NUEVO ORDEN

Soundbed: Generic advertising jingles.

SERIOUS-SOUNDING LATINO MALE VOICE:
"good evening x-timados radiobedientes
this is your noticiero de fin de siglo
1,000 megahertz above reality
at the top of the news tonight:
ex-president Bush has been diagnosed with Downs syndrome
Pinochet falls but leaves a triple shadow behind
Superbarrio replaces Boutros Ghali at the United Nations
the Dalai Lama relocates to El Salvador
the Eastern bloc goes West . . . for shopping
Gorbachev confesses he was just kidding
American artists demand gringostroika at home
Canada adopts Japanese as the only official language
Panamá invades Washington in search of Oliver North
Saddam is seen with Margaret Thatcher in Saint Tropez
Violeta Chamorro is photographed naked at an S&M party
— the only woman in an ocean of Sandinista studs
the pope & the king of Spain prepare for the Mother of all Fiestas:
the rediscovery and recolonization of the Americas
this time, cosponsored by CNN, Televisa, & Goya Products
the pope confesses he contracted AIDS during his recent trip to Brazil

AIDS has finally affected the immuno-logical system of the mainstream
the Heritage Foundation censors this un-American broad . . .
(radio static interrupts the broadcast)
multiculturalism becomes a nostalgic TV series
(radio static again)
tonight, the Art World discovers a new "ism"
meta, post, infra, beta, plus, et cetera . . . et cetera . . . et cetera . . .
(the sound is lost to interference for about 15 seconds)
. . . a Japanese artist invents a new audio system . . .
(the transmission is interrupted by a female voice)
FEMALE TECHNO-ALTERED VOICE (W/DELAY):
you can listen to the voice of your other selves
& to the voices of your ancestors
you can push a button
& transfer your voice to image
or vice versa (you don't need to know why, or how to do it)
you don't have to go out anymore
you don't even need to make art or read
OUR syntax has been simplified to meet your psycho-cultural needs
remember,
MY literature is as simple as a newscast
remember,
your personal needs are OUR global challenge
good evening, this is SU noticiero de fin the siglo
1,000 megahertz above reality

A commercial for Free Trade Art begins.

Right: Anthropologist with a group of natives (note his left hand). Photo courtesy
of "The Year of the White Bear," Fusco/Gómez-Peña archives

colonial dreams/
post-colonial nightmares

COLONIAL DREAMS/POST—COLONIAL NIGHTMARES
A Chronicle of Performance Projects (1979—1995)

I AM A CITIZEN OF TWO COUNTRIES, A MEMBER OF MULTIPLE COMMUNI-
ties, and a stubborn practitioner of many disciplines. Like many
members of my generation, I wear different hats (or masks) at different times, and sometimes more than one at once. I am variously an
activist artist, a border pirate, and/or a cross-cultural citizen diplomat,
performing the temporary and ever-changing roles of reversed anthropologist, experimental linguist, alternative chronicler, and reformist
within the Unites States' cultural institutions.

In my art I explore the labyrinths of identity, the intersections of
language, and the precipices of nationality. Both my psyche and my performance stage are X-rays of the continental map, and my body is at
times a laboratory for experimentation, or an exotic specimen on display,
a pagan creature debating between martyrdom and transcendence, or a
monster to be redeemed and, if necessary, destroyed.

I have embarked on a long-term project: to make relentlessly
experimental — yet accessible — art; to work in politically/emotionally
charged sites and for diverse audiences; and to always collaborate across
racial, gender, and age boundaries as a gesture of citizen diplomacy. My
work makes sense only in relation to that of my colleagues. We cross
many dangerous borders together, and in doing so we risk our identity,
our dignity, and sometimes, our lives.

In this chronicle of my performance work, I have chosen to outline primarily those projects which took place in contexts outside of the "art world" — public places, historically charged buildings and monuments, shopping malls, natural history museums, cyber-space, etc. Those which were performed within the boundaries of the art world utilized the gallery space as a fictional location, and not as the usual "neutral zone."

Gómez-Peña as a colonial mestizo. Mexico City performance, 1979.

The Loneliness of the Immigrant (1979)

A few months after my arrival in Los Angeles, I spent twenty-four hours in a public elevator, wrapped in Indian fabric and tied into a bundle with rope. I was unable to move or to talk back. My total anonymity and vulnerability seemed to grant people the freedom to confess intimate things to me (things I didn't want to hear), to verbally abuse me, and to kick me. I overheard two adolescents discuss the possibility of setting me on fire, a dog peed on me, and finally, the security guards threw me into an industrial trash can, where I spent the last two hours of the day.

To me, this piece was a metaphor of painful birth into a new country, a new identity — Chicano — and a new language — intercultural performance. I quote from my performance diaries: *"As a new immigrant, I hope this piece will help to transform insensitive views on immigration. In one way or another, we all are, or will be, immigrants. Surely one day we will be able to crack this shell, this incommensurable loneliness, and develop a transcontinental identity."*

As part of the same series, I laid for twelve hours on the streets as a "homeless person," as an expression of the despair and loneliness felt by a newly arrived immigrant. Despite the fact that I was wrapped in a *zarape* and surrounded by candles and various personal belongings, most people ignored me. I discovered that as a Mexican (and as a homeless person), I was literally invisible to California's Anglo population. In my next performance, I felt compelled to scream at the top of my lungs over the Los Angeles skyscrapers: *"Deal with me! I am here to stay! Fucking deal with me! See my people all around you! See yourself in me, in my people, in our collective pain! Deal with us! We are here to stay!"*

Spanglish Poetry Reading in a Public Bathroom (Cal Arts, 1979)

This piece was another attempt to bring performance and language into unusual contexts, and to disrupt people's sense of the quotidian. For twenty-four hours, I sat on a toilet and read aloud epic poetry describing my journey to the United States. Whoever happened to come into the bathroom — for whatever reason — experienced the piece.

Through this and other experiments of its kind, I became interested in the notion of performing for "involuntary audiences."

Mexiphobia: Postrevolutionary Situations (1980)

Most Americans perceive Mexicans through the distorted lens of Hollywood, and the stereotypes of pop and mass culture: To them, we are mythical creatures who inhabit a landscape of fear and desire.

In 1980, I was busted by the L.A. police for looking "suspicious," meaning for being a Mexican. I began to experiment with cultural fear. I took certain stereotypes about Mexico and Mexicans, stylized them, exaggerated them, and then inserted them back into public spaces. My friends and I began to show up at various places dressed as caricatures of "typical drug dealers," "illegal aliens," and "bandidos" (mariachis with our faces covered with bandanas or Mexican wrestling masks); yet we would behave in ways that would defy the stereotype. Once, I ate at a fancy restaurant dressed as a "typical Latino terrorist." The place emptied out within five minutes of my arrival.

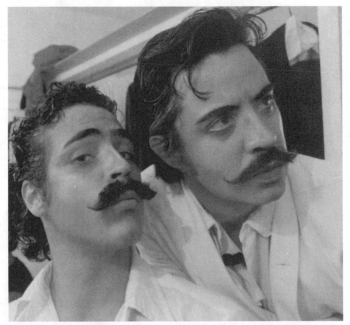

"The Two Mr. Misterios" Leonides Guadarrama and Gómez-Peña as performance twins. Los Angeles, 1980

Proto–multicultural experiments: Poyesis Genética (1981–1984)

In 1981 at Cal Arts, choreographer Sara-Jo Berman and I formed an interdisciplinary arts collective named "Poyesis Genética" (from the Spanish *pollo* — a derogative term used in the Southwest for migrant workers — not from the Greek *poiesis*). Its members were mostly U.S. artists of color and newly arrived immigrants from Latin America, Europe, the Middle East, and Canada, bound by a shared sense of cultural displacement. Our objective was (I quote from an early brochure): "to develop syncretic languages capable of articulating our unstable condition as cultural outsiders and aesthetic freaks."

We began to explore the notion of a growing Third World culture within the shrinking First World. We also addressed issues of nostalgia, memory, language, homeland, and nationality, and the interactive role that these factors play in the formation and continuous (re)creation of transitional and multiple identities. I rapidly learned that to be a "Mexican artist" in the United States meant — whether I liked it or not — being a member of a culture of resistance; and that the art I was making was perceived by the art world as "minor," "peripheral," and intellectually unsophisticated. I also realized that as a Mexican in the process of Chicanization I might have more in common with other people of color living in the United States than with other Mexicans who never left Mexico.

In terms of artistic strategies, we began to fuse our various cultural traditions, utilizing performance as a syntactic thread. We mixed indigenous rituals from various parts of the world (or rather, our personal interpretations of them) with film and video. We combined social chronicle and multilingual poetry, art and literature, sexual and political imagery; and we performed indiscriminately in art spaces, theaters, and in the streets. We often used live animals onstage, slow-motion movement, nudity, and body paint; and experimented with what we believed were altered states of consciousness, induced either by fasting, overeating, alcohol, or lack of sleep.

Photo courtesy of Poyesis Genética archives

In 1983, after spending six months in Europe performing mainly in artists' lofts and in the streets, Poyesis relocated to the Tijuana/San Diego border region, and there we found an ideal terrain to explore intercultural relations. Our work became more overtly political. We began to use the border art technique of recycling (border culture is by nature one of recyclement). The idea was to bring radical performance imagery into other, multiple contexts — an image from a live performance might become a photo-mural, a poster, a T-shirt, a conceptual postcard, a velvet painting, or an illustration for a magazine, thus transforming its objective and also its value.

The Velvet Hall of Fame (ongoing)

Since the mid-'80s, I have been collaborating with velvet painters from Tijuana, mainly with Jorge T. and Beto Ruíz. I provide

Performance intersects with cinema. Louis Malle "shoots" Gómez-Peña at the Centro Cultural de la Raza, San Diego, 1986. Photo by Philip Brookman

them with drafts and photos of my performance and literary characters and they interpret them, painting on velvet in the traditional "tourist arts" style. The process is very matter-of-fact — the more I pay, the better the painting is, period. They don't care about art reviews or openings, but they get a kick out of my particular madness.

My involvement with "conceptual velvet art" stems from an obsession: I love the idea of pop and tourist culture invading the sacred temples of high art. The idea of exhibiting velvet art and recontextualized tourist artifacts at the Corcoran Gallery or the Detroit Institute for the Arts, for example, is simply irresistible. When I see these paintings hanging at walking distance from a Van Gogh or a David Salle, I somehow feel historically vindicated.

Border Arts Workshop/Taller de Arte Fronterizo (1984 –1990)

In 1984, a group of Chicano, Mexicano, and Anglo artists got together to form a binational arts collective, BAW/TAF. Our objective was to explore U.S.-Mexico relations and border issues through performance, video, installation art, and experimental poetry. We proclaimed the border region "a laboratory for social and aesthetic experimentation," and proposed "the artist as a social thinker and binational diplomat." Similar activist groups formed in other parts of the country (i.e., Grand Fury, The Guerrilla Girls, LAPD, etc.). It was the spirit of the times — performance, political activism, and community concerns were completely intertwined.

In addition to art exhibitions, bilingual publications, radio programs, and town meetings, BAW/TAF organized performance events right at the border — where the U.S. meets Mexico at the Pacific Ocean — literally performing for audiences in both countries. If the U.S. border patrol came too close, we crossed to the Mexican side, and vice versa. During some performances, we invited our audiences to cross to the other side "illegally." We exchanged food and art "illegally," caressed and kissed "illegally" across the border fence, and confronted the border patrol in character. We were always protected by the presence of friendly journalists and video cameras. The political implications of the site and the symbolism of our actions garnered immediate media attention and, as Robert Sanchez said, "took us from the calendar section to the political section of the papers." In 1988, Emily Hicks and I staged a "performance wedding" on the borderline. The media labeled the event "a masterpiece of symbolic politics."

BAW/TAF also did work in art spaces; these strictly artistic activities helped to "legitimize" our more activist work and protected our collective back. Two projects come to mind:

In "911" (La Jolla Museum of Contemporary Art, 1987), BAW/TAF transformed the gallery into a bizarre border house. The floor, walls, and roof were slightly crooked, with video monitors for windows. On the dining table, instead of food, we served news — video monitors under the plates played collages of sensationalist news about Mexico. The objective was to express how fear of otherness defines most social and cultural transactions between the two countries, and yet how Mexico is so present and so much a part of California's everyday life.

In early 1989, at Artists' Space (New York), members of the workshop created several installations. My favorite was Robert Sanchez's: A macabre ritual space with containers of pesticides and fertilizers, red flowers, and ultraviolet lights, it was a direct reference to the fields of California. The idea was to create a beautiful, meditative space which was also dangerous, to reveal the contradictions of a "utopia" built with the blood and sweat of migrant workers.

In 1990, most of the original members left the workshop and a new group was formed.[1]

Documented/Undocumented (1986–1987)

While a member of BAW/TAF, I was also doing solo pieces and collaborative projects with other artists. In 1986–87, Emily Hicks and I created a series of site-specific performances titled "Documented/Undocumented." We were playing with the term's double application, both to immigration status and to an ephemeral art piece. The characters in this series were constantly walking that line back and forth. The performances were staged for the camera, and documented in photojournalistic style.

In the following photo, for example, a Latin American general in exile somewhere in La Jolla or on Coronado Island performs for his inner ghosts and troubling memories. The actual site of the performance was in a house right next to a military base in Imperial Beach, California.

---

[1] For more information on BAW/TAF's border performances, see the two catalogs published by the Centro Cultural de la Raza (San Diego).

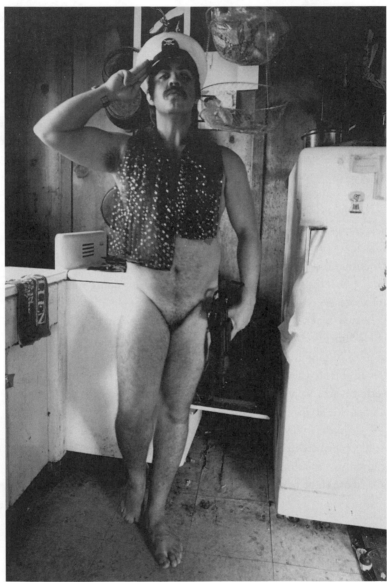

From the series "Documented/Undocumented." Photo by Henri Witkowski

Tijuana-Niagara (1988)

In 1988, Emily and I spent a month on a "performance pilgrimage," working along the U.S./Canadian border between Ontario and New York State, with Art Park as our base of operations. We travelled in a mobile temple, made of psuedo-indigenous souveniers and religious kitsch purchased in both Tijuana and Niagara Falls.

We carried out fifteen "performance actions" such as: auctions of border art (border art must be auctioned), "spiritual consultations for tourists," photo sessions with "authentic border shamans and witches," begging for money in costume, and broadcasting bilingual poetry with a huge megaphone from one shore of the Niagara River to the other. We were commenting on the commodification of ethnicity by the tourist industries of border towns.

During that period, my collaborators and I staged many other performance pilgrimages in different U.S.-Mexico border cities.

Emily Hicks and Gómez-Peña in "Tijuana-Niagara." Photo by Biff Hendricks

The Birth of Border Brujo (1988)

Once, performance artist Hugo Sánchez and I crossed the border checkpoint in costume. I was dressed as the "Border Brujo" and Hugo as "El Pipila," carrying a stone slab made out of papier-mâché on his back. After an hour-long interrogation, we were finally allowed into the United States Then, we walked approximately eighteen kilometers from San Ysidro to San Diego's Balboa Park. That night, Hugo and I did a performance in which we "exchanged our identities."

From 1988 to 1992, I attempted to cross the border in costume several times. I was rejected three times, and those rejected personae never found their way into my performances.

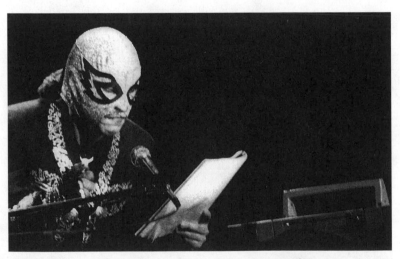

Performance monologue at The Space, Boston. Photo courtesy of The Space

Right: Gómez-Peña as a cultural transvestite. ICA, Boston, 1991

The Migrant Artist (1988–1991)

By 1988, many of us felt that performance had become so artificial and technically complex that we needed to get back to the basics. The result was a low-tech, language-based, and highly politicized "performance monologue" movement. This provided incredible mobility, both geographical (one could travel easily, with the entire production fitting into a suitcase), as well as among disciplines (work could be presented in the various contexts of art, theater, literature, education, and radio). Precisely because of this, performance became a very eclectic milieu — the field slowly expanded to include spoken-word poets, eccentric theater monologists, radical theoreticians, disenchanted journalists, and stand-up comedians.

My most significant piece during this period was "Border Brujo," a multilingual monologue dealing with identity and border issues. With this piece, I became a migrant performance artist. I spent two years on the road, going from community to community, from city to city, from country to

Angelica Rivera, Bart Uchida, Debbie Sanchez-Reed, and Gómez-Peña collaborate in a performance jamming session at The Space, Boston, 1991. Photo by Charles Mayer

country, reproducing the migratory patterns of the Mexican diaspora. As I traveled, I incorporated information, images, props, and costumes into the piece. The Brujo and I finally ended up back at the U.S.-Mexico border; there I buried his costume and props and staged a performance funeral.

By the early '90s, the performance monologue movement had become extremely fashionable. There were thousands of self-proclaimed performance artists all over the country — people who felt that to confess a personal trauma or to tell a strident anecdote about their victimization onstage constituted performance art. The field had also entirely overlapped with bad stand-up comedy and character acting. It was time to do something else.

Segregating the Audience (1991–1993)

In 1990, I began to collaborate with writer and artist Coco Fusco. In some proscenium pieces ("The '1992' Trilogy" and "The New World Border"), we introduced the performance strategy of "segregating" the audience as it entered the theater, utilizing various criteria: a person's degree of bilingualism, racial background, immigration status, and/or their position vis-à-vis certain political issues. Sometimes members of "ethnic minorities," immigrants, and bilingual audience members would be allowed to enter the theater first and to take the best seats. At other times, we would seat "bilinguals, people of color, and immigrants" on one side of the theater, and "the rest" on the other. Even interracial couples would sometimes have to sit in different parts of the theater.

"Privileged" audience members — those who could understand the bi- or trilingual texts and also the cultural specificities — felt empowered, and didn't hesitate to express their approval of our experiment during the show. In doing so, they made the "others" — the monolingual "Anglos" — feel "excluded" and marginalized. The idea was to create a fictional center which we would occupy for the duration of the performance, thereby forcing monolingual/monocultural Americans to feel like outsiders and "minorities" in their own country, even if only for an hour or two. Understandably, this artificial inversion of the social and

Coco Fusco as "Miss Discovery" segregating the audience before
a performance at the Randolph Street Gallery, Chicago, 1993.
Photo courtesy of Randolph Street Gallery

racial pyramid of U.S. society generated a very tense dynamic among the
audience members. At the end of each performance we would have a discussion, which often turned into a very heated town meeting.

Performance as reversed anthropology: The Guatinaui World Tour (1992–1993)

In 1992, during the heated Columbus debates, Coco Fusco and I
decided to remind the United States and Europe of "the other history of
intercultural performance": the human exhibits, pseudo-ethnographic
tableaux vivants, and the living dioramas that were so popular in Europe
from the 17th through the early 20th century — and that in the U.S.

evolved into more vulgar versions, such as the dime museum and the freak show. In all cases, the premise was similar: "Authentic primitives" were exhibited as human artifacts and mythical specimens in cages, taverns, gardens, salons, and fairs, as well as in museums of ethnography and natural history, often next to samples of their homeland's flora and fauna, with costumes and ritual artifacts that were designed by the impresario and had little or nothing to do with reality. This sinister practice contributed a great deal to the formation of European and American mythologies about the New World's inhabitants and, sadly, many of these misperceptions are still evident in contemporary mass media and pop cultural depictions of the Latino "other."

The meta-fiction of "The Guatinaui World Tour" was as follows: Coco and I lived for three-day periods in a gilded cage, on exhibition as "undiscovered Amerindians" from the (fictional) island of Guatinau (Spanglishization of "what now"). I was dressed as a kind of Aztec wrestler from Las Vegas, and Coco as a Taina straight out of *Gilligan's Island*. We were hand-fed by fake museum docents, and taken to the bathroom on leashes. Taxonomic plates describing our costumes and physical characteristics were displayed next to the cage.

Besides performing "authentic rituals," we would write on a laptop computer, watch home videos of our native land, and listen to Latin American rock music on a boom box. For a modest amount, we would perform "authentic" Guatinaui dances, and chant or tell stories in our (made-up) Guatinaui language. Visitors also had the option to take a souvenir snapshot with the primitives. For the '93 Whitney Biennial, we added another activity to the menu: for $5.00, the audience could "see the genitals of the male specimen" — and the well-heeled Whitney patrons really went for it.

We brought this performance to Columbus Plaza in Madrid, London's Covent Garden, the Smithsonian Institution in Washington, the Field Museum of Chicago, New York's Whitney Museum of American Art, the Australia Museum in Sydney, and the Fundación Banco

"The Guatinaui World Tour." Coco Fusco and Gómez-Peña on display in Madrid's Columbus Plaza, 1992. Photo by Peter Barker

Patricios in Buenos Aires. As it traveled from site to site, it became more stylized, staged, and whimsical. Sadly, over 40 percent of our audience, no matter where we were, believed that the exhibit was real (at least during their first visit), and did not feel compelled to do anything about it.

Experimental archeology: The Year of the White Bear (1992)

"The Year of the White Bear" premiered in October 1992 at the Walker Art Center in Minneapolis and then it went to Chicago (Mexican Fine Arts Center) and Los Angeles (Otis Parsons Gallery). With this installation piece, Coco and I parodied the blockbuster multi-cultural shows of the early '90s, revealing their inherent political contradictions by juxtaposing "authentic" pre-Columbian and colonial art and artifacts with trashy tourist artifacts and contemporary art. Again, we adopted a fictional center, and pushed the dominant culture to the margins, treating it as exotic and unfamiliar. Among other installations, we (re)created "an excavation site of tourists from Wisconsin, after being raided by angry locals," and "a British collector's room" with his "secret collection" of stolen indigenous artifacts, revealing his interracial sexual fantasies. Our museum labels in simulated academic jargon revealed important information about the way the objects were obtained, and about the political implications of "naming" other cultures. Through these exhibits, Coco and I began a dialogue with radical anthropologists and cultural critics working on parallel projects.

Performing in malls: Mexarcane International (1994–1995)

My last collaboration with Coco Fusco consisted of a series of performances called "Mexarcane International (Ethnic Talent for Export)." We invented "a (fictional) post-NAFTA multinational corporation to market and distribute ethnic talent worldwide" and brought it to shopping malls, placing our exhibition stand and temporary "office" in a highly visible site, usually next to the foodcourt. A corporate-style backdrop — complete with explanatory texts in imitation corporate language, and happy images of exotic primitives from around the world — was set up behind a desk at which Coco would be seated; across from her, approximately ten meters away, was my cage.

For four to six hours a day, over three-day periods, I exhibited myself inside a small gilded or bamboo cage as an exotic multicultural specimen (every detail and motif in my costume came from a different culture in the Americas). I was "a living sample of Mexarcane's products for export," and visitors to the mall could "activate me" to experience firsthand my "incredible ethnic talents." My "live demonstrations" included: doing a commercial for chile shampoo and other organic products; modeling tribal wear; posing in attitudes of martyrdom, despair, and poverty "for German documentary photographers and U.S. evange-lists"; doing shamanistic rituals "for confused suburbanites"; playing New Age tribal music concerts (on toy instruments); and demonstrating "pre-Columbian condoms," using a clay dildo as a proxy. During these demonstrations, Coco Fusco (who was dressed as the Aztec girlfriend of Mr. Spock) conducted interviews and surveys to determine the "ethnic desires" of the audience. After each interview, she would decide which "demonstration" was fit for a particular consumer, who was then asked to approach the composite Indian (myself) and ask him to "perform."

This project was first tested at the National Review of Live Arts (Glasgow), and then it was taken to Toronto's Dufferin Mall and to London's elegant Whiteleys Shopping Center as part of LIFT '95.

Living and dying dioramas: The Shame-man Meets El Mexican't (1993–ongoing)

James Luna and I have known each other since the mid-'80s, and though our work is stylistically quite different, we share similar con-cerns. We are both critical of the way indigenous identities are por-trayed by mainstream cultural institutions and commodified by pop culture, tourism, and self-realization movements. Since 1992, we have engaged in one collaborative project per year under the title "The Shame-man Meets El Mexican't at (name of the host organization)." One project comes to mind, and I quote from my performance diaries:

It's Friday morning. Luna and I share a diorama space at the Smithsonian's Museum of Natural History. I sit on a toilet dressed as a mari-achi in a straitjacket with a sign around my neck that reads "There used to be a Mexican inside this body." I attempt unsuccessfully to get rid of my straitjacket in order to "perform" ("entertain" or "educate" my audience). James paces back and forth, changing identities. At times he is an "Indian shoe-shiner." Other times he becomes a "diabetic Indian," shooting insulin directly into his stomach. He then transforms into a janitor of color (like most of the janitors in this, and other museums) and vacuums the diorama floor. Hundreds of visitors gather in front of us. They are sad, very sad and perplexed. Next to us, the "real" Indian dioramas speak of a mute world outside of history and social crises, and next to us, they strangely appear to be much less "authentic." The visibly nervous staff makes sure that the audience understands that "this is just performance art."

"El Shame-man Meets El Mexican't at the Smithsonian Motel and Golf Course." Gómez-Peña and James Luna, 1993. (Note: This photo was rejected for promotional purposes by the museum's publicity department because "it suggests a homoerotic relationship between Gómez-Peña and Luna.")
Photo by Cristina Taccone

Intergenerational Collaboration (ongoing)

My work with Roberto Sifuentes dates back to 1991, when he was the technical director of my "1991" performance project at the Next Wave Festival (Brooklyn Academy of Music), and for the past three years he has been my main collaborator. Two important borders separate us: cultural and generational. He is a Chicano in the process of Mexicanization and I am a Mexican in the process of Chicanization. He is eleven years my junior. These borders have become the raw material of our performance investigations.

Performing for the media: The Cruci-fiction Project (1994)

In early '94, Roberto and I crucified ourselves for three hours on sixteen-foot-high crosses at Rodeo Beach (in front of San Francisco's Golden Gate Bridge. The piece was designed for the media, as a symbolic protest against the xenophobic immigration politics of California's governor Pete Wilson. Inspired by the biblical myth of Dimas and Gestas (two petty thieves who were cruficied alongside of Jesus), Roberto and I decided to dress as "two contemporary public enemies of California": I was an "undocumented bandido," crucified by the INS [Immigration and Naturalization Service], and Roberto was a generic "gang member," crucified by the LAPD [Los Angeles Police Department].

Our audience of over 300 people each received a handout, asking them to "free us from our martyrdom as a gesture of political commitment." However, we had miscalculated their response. Paralyzed by the melancholia of the image, it took them over three hours to figure out how to get us down. By then, my right shoulder had become dislocated and Roberto had passed out. We were carried to a nearby bonfire and nurtured back to reality, while some people in the crowd rebuked those who were trying to help us, saying, "Let them die!"

Gómez-Peña and Roberto Sifuentes in "The Cruci-fiction Project." Marin Headlands, 1994. Photo by Neph Navas

Photographs of the event were quickly picked up by the media, and the piece became international news. The image appeared in, among other publications, *Der Speigel* (Germany), *Cambio 16* (Spain), *Reforma* and *La Jornada* (Mexico), and various U.S. newspapers. The photos have since reappeared in major news media and art publications as the debates on immigration and arts funding continue to be the focus of the political right. Last month someone showed me another fate of one of those photos: It had been turned into a greeting card.

Performance as a "false" religion: The Temple of Confessions (1994–ongoing)

In this performance/installation, Roberto and I combine the format of the pseudo-ethnographic diorama (like my prior work with Fusco and Luna) with that of the religious dioramas often displayed in colonial Mexican churches. For three-day periods, we exhibit ourselves in plexiglass boxes as both "holy creatures" and "cultural specimens," calling ourselves "end-of-the-century saints." The Temple functions at the same time as an elaborate set design for a theater of mythos, and a melancholy ceremonial space for people to reflect on their attitudes toward other cultures. There are three main areas, the "Chapel of Desires," the "Chapel of Fears," and a mortuary chamber in the middle.

In the "Chapel of Desires," Roberto is on display as "El Pre-Columbian Vato," a "holy gang member" engaged in slow-motion, ritualized actions. His arms and face are painted with pre-Columbian tattoos, and his T-shirt is covered with blood and holes from gunshots. He shares his plexiglass box with fifty cockroaches, a live four-foot-long iguana, and a small table covered with useless technological gadgets and what appear to be real weapons. Behind him stands a façade of a pre-Columbian temple.

Opposite Roberto in the "Chapel of Fears," I sit in a wheelchair or on a toilet, dressed as "San Pocho Aztlaneca," a hyper-exoticized "curio shop shaman for spiritual tourists." Dozens of tourist souvenirs and tribal talismans hang from my "Tex-Mex/Aztec" outfit. I share my plexiglass box with live crickets, a taxidermied chicken, tribal musical instruments, and a table filled with witchcraft-looking artifacts. My altar is framed by neon.

In the middle gallery, visitors encounter an enigmatic vignette: a six-foot-tall wooden Indian and a mannequin wrapped in leopard skin mourn the contents of a body bag stamped by the INS. Velvet paintings depicting other hybrid saints hang on the red and black walls leading to the living *santos*. Underneath each painting, a small table holds votive candles and assorted symbolic objects. People are encouraged to light a candle and to deposit personal *ofrendas* on the tables. "chola-nuns"

(Norma Medina, Michelle Ceballos, and Carmel Kooros) perform the dual roles of caretakers of the Temple and living icons. At times they are mere frozen images; other times, they chant Mexican religious songs, clean the plexiglass boxes, or approach audience members to encourage them to "confess." Their tableaux comment on classical painting, Catholic imagery, and movie stereotypes.

Those visitors who wish to "confess" their intercultural fears and desires to the "living saints" have three options: They can either confess into the microphones placed on kneelers in front of the plexiglass boxes (their voices are recorded, and then altered in postproduction to ensure their anonymity); or, if they are shy, they can write their confessons on a card and deposit them in an urn, or call an 800 number. The most revealing confessions are later edited into the gallery soundtrack for future performances.

By the end of the third day, we leave the plexiglass boxes and are replaced by life-size effigies. The Temple remains as an installation for the next three to six weeks. Written and phone confessions are still accepted.

So far, the Temple has been presented at the Scottsdale Center for the Arts (Arizona), the Three Rivers Arts Festival (Pittsburgh), the Detroit Institute of Arts, Ex-Teresa Arte Alternativo (Mexico City), the Bannister Art Gallery (Providence), and it will be presented at the Corcoran Gallery in November of '96.

El Shame-man and El Mexican't Meet Cybervato at the Ethno-Cyberpunk Trading Post & Curio Shop on the Electronic Frontier (1995)

In this collaborative performance/installation, Roberto, James Luna, and I spent five days living/performing inside the Diverseworks gallery space in San Antonio. Commenting on the multiple roles of the artist in the end of the century, we revealed the transformation processes that go from the realm of the personal to the public, and from ritual space to cyberspace.

As visitors moved through the gallery, they found a "dressing room area," where we applied our makeup and changed costumes; a simulated "high art area," where our props and personal objects, along with various folk, pre-Columbian, and pop cultural artifacts were carefully displayed as aestheticized museum pieces (with labels that changed daily); finally arriving at a "human exhibition area," where we displayed ourselves as exotic "cultural specimens" and "performance artists at work." Various monitors throughout the gallery played B-movies with racist depictions of Indians and Mexicans, as well as trashy TV broadcasts, i.e., evangelist preachers, the home shopping channel, and local news broadcasts.

Each day, in front of the visitors, James and I transformed ourselves into different performance personae. Roberto captured the details of these transformations on a video camera, and these images were shown simultaneously on the gallery's video monitors and were also transmitted live onto the Internet.

Parallel to this process, Roberto exhibited himself as "Cyber-Vato," a living diorama of a highly technified "gang member" consumed by techno-gadgetry and weapons. He had state-of-the-art technology to transmit daily messages to the World Wide Web, and he was connected to satellite sites at Rice University and MECA, via video teleconferencing. Internet users who visited our Web page were invited to send in images and/or texts about how they felt Mexicans and Native Americans should look, behave, and perform in the '90s. These texts, images, and sounds were shown on monitors manipulated by Cyber-Vato, and they were also incorporated into the changing personae created by James and I. In a sense, we were ethno-cyborgs, created by the imaginations of the Net users.

By the third day, the Shame-man as a human artifact was replaced by local artists and adventurous audience members, who got to wear Luna's costumes and become "a real Indian" for a period of time. On the fifth day, Roberto and I left the gallery space and ventured into the city in costume to stage a series of "public actions." The installation remained on view for six more weeks, and the techno-interaction continued through the run of the show.

"Performero. They threw me out of the Museum of Anthropology. I didn't find a job in Hollywood. No one believes that I'm a Zapatista." Ex-Teresa Arte Alternativo, Mexico City, 1995. Photo by Monica Naranjo

And the Show Goes On . . .

As far as I can see into the future, I perceive three options regarding my artwork. First, to continue my performative exploration of intercultural relations and "reversed anthropology," both in art spaces and in the more populist venues where nonspecialized audiences can be exposed to socially conscious, experimental art. Second, Roberto and I have already begun to incorporate some of the new technologies (an Internet component, a Web page, and a CD-ROM) into our performance work, and we are interested in pursuing this in a responsible,

The San Francisco cartel for "Borderama": Darryl Bates, Sara Shelton Mann, Darren Chase, Margaret Leonard, Roberto Sifuentes, Gómez-Peña, and Eric Pukprayura. Theater Artaud, 1996. Photo by Eugenio Castro

innovative way. We are currently developing a series of high-tech performance projects that deal with desire and fear of otherness, immigration, and race relations. These projects involve humor and multilingualism, with a meta-language that questions matters of access and privilege. Finally, I feel it is important to continue creating "ephemeral communities" that bring artists together to work intensely on a common goal for a short period of time, as we did with the "Borderama" series and also in "Terreno Peligroso/Danger Zone."

The unprecedented (and perhaps irreversible) political, cultural, and economic crisis that is afflicting our continent is forcing artists and intellectuals to reevaluate our working methods, our communication strategies, and even our roles in society. In the United States, where xenophobia, conservatism, and isolationism have become accepted as part of mainstream culture, the "alternative space" network is literally crumbling, and funding sources for art are cautious and scarce. It has become much more difficult to carry out large-scale projects of a collaborative nature, especially those involving artists from other countries. And paradoxically, the work we are doing seems more pertinent than ever. I firmly believe that despite the indifference (and in some cases, overt antagonism) of the political class, the role that art and education can perform is crucial and irreplaceable.

NAFTAZTEC: PIRATE CYBER-TV FOR A.D. 2000

O N THANKSGIVING DAY 1994, THE EVENING NEWS OF OVER 3.5 million American households was interrupted by two "cyber-Aztec TV pirates," transmitting bizarre views on American culture and identity "direct from their underground vato-bunker, somewhere between New York, Miami, and Los Angeles."

In actuality, what the viewers were witnessing was an experiment in interactive television via satellite. Roberto Sifuentes and I had teamed with filmmakers Adrienne Jenik, Philip Djwa, and Branda Miller (from iEar Studio at Rensselaer Polytechnic Institute) to broadcast a simulacrum of a pirate TV intervention to hundreds of cable television stations across the country. The stations' program directors had agreed to play along, and had advertised the time slot under a fictional title. From time to time during the broadcast, it would appear that the TV station was struggling to regain the airwaves, but then we would manage to retain control.

For an hour and a half, the "cyber bandits" encouraged perplexed viewers to call in and respond to the broadcast, which was a strange blend of radical politics, autobiographical material, and parodies — traditional TV formats gone bananas. The visual style was very much like MTV, with five handheld cameras in constant motion. We spoke in English, Spanglish, French, and a type of esperanto, and we asked our viewers "to be intelligent, poetic, and performative" in their responses. We demonstrated a "Chicano virtual reality machine," and received "live reports" via PictureTel (video telephone) from the Electronic Café in Santa Monica, California. The performance was also transmitted over computer networks via "M-Bone," and those watching in cyberspace could interact with us, and with each other, by posting written and visual comments. We received dozens of phone calls and computer messages.

What follows are two excerpts from the broadcast.

A newscast is in progress, when suddenly it is interrupted by static. Graffiti-style calligraphy fills the screen:

A TV INTERVENCIÓN PIRATA

Then, a Wrestler/Shaman appears on the screen, speaking in tongues.

Scroll:

THE WRESTLER/SHAMAN ADDRESSES A PERPLEXED TV AUDI-ENCE IN HIS PERSONAL ESPERANTO. BRIEF MISTRANSLATION: "ESTIMADO TELEVIDENTE, DO YOU FEEL LIKE A FOREIGNER IN YOUR OWN COUNTRY?"

Camera pans out to El Naftazteca and Cyber-Vato in the television studio. The set is straight out of a '60s Mexican sci-fi movie. El Cyber-Vato appears to be crucified to the TV equipment.

El Naftazteca: *(live on screen, grabs a maraca microphone)* Good evening post-NAFTA America. I'm sorry to inform you that this is a pirate TV broadcast. My name is El Naf-taz-tec: cross-cultural salesman, disc-jockey apocalíptico, and information superhighway bandido, all in one, within, & vice versa, interrupting your coitus, as always. With me tonight are East Los techno-gang member Cyber-Vato, and three dead chickens donated by my Aunt Rosa.

Camera No. 2, please get those pinche pajaros down there, s'il vous plait. *(camera captures the chickens running amok in the vato-bunker)*

We were going to sacrifice a live chicken on the set, but the crew threatened to desert us, so we decided to spare his life.

Tonight, you are about to witness a miracle of techno-ras-cuachismo, a true example of post-CNN Chicano Art, ¿que qué?! ¡Yeesss! an interactive TV program, never before shown in the western world. Yes, I will demonstrate live on national television my Chicano virtual reality machine. With this new system, called TECHNOPAL 2000, I can turn my memories into video images, ipso facto, meaning that I can retrieve any episode of my life, any performance I was ever involved in, any persona or hidden self that exists within me, or any historical event involving my family and my raza — the Chicano/Mexicano communities in the U.S. — ¿que qué? Oui messieur, and on top of that, I can edit these memories on the spot and turn them into video footage, like so. *(snaps his fingers)*

No mames. How? Simply by rotating my tribal antennae or by pressing a button. Yes, it's all digital, essse . . . Inter-ac-ti-voooo-dooo Verbigratia. *(turns knobs on control panel)*

Scroll:

WHO IS OUT THERE? CALL IN AND TELL US YOUR REAL AND YOUR DESIRED AGE, RACE, PROFESSION, AND GENDER. 818-276-4778

*Voiceover (**Cyber-Vato**):*

Qui est la? Appellez et dites nous votre age, race, profession, gender, vrai ou desirec.

Live on screen:

Cyber-Vato dissects the back of the set. He opens the computers with a knife and eats the insides.

El Naftazteca: *(back on screen, manipulating a small, unrecognizable machine)* Oui, culeros. For the next hour and a half, you will have direct access to the labyrinthic mind of a Mexican — and not just any Mexican, but one who talks back, can you believe it? An illegal Mexican performance artist with unlimited access to state-of-the-art technology, live on national television!! This is a historical day, but there's only one problem. Our system still doesn't have translation capabilities, and it's not perfected yet for Spanglish, which means there won't be any accents or tildes in our scrolls. We are currently beta-testing the TECHNOPAL 2000. During my demonstration of this amazing machine, I encourage you to call the following number & tell me what YOU think, if you think anything at all.

Hablo, ergo, chingo, jodo, veo, meo, por lo tanto existo. . . .

(the telephone rings)

Phone Call: Too much blah-blah, man. I want to see if it's true. I want to see something from Aztec times. Can you do that?

El Naftazteca: *(speaking into his watch)* Sure. Let's go back to the golden age of multiculturalism. While you watch the following video memory, I want you to remember one thing: We are merely mythical creatures created by your cultural fears and erotic desires. *(sinister laughter)* Our video-memories will soon also be yours. *(he turns to address the camera)* Yes, gabachos, American identity is a messy business, ¿que no? *(he howls and turns knobs on the control panel)*

Letters appear on screen:
PART 1: "A BRIEF HISTORY OF PERFORMANCE ART"

Scroll:
>JUEGO DE PELOTA. INVOLUNTARY PERFORMANCE EXTRAVA-GANZA, HOLLYWOOD-TENOCHTITLÁN, CIRCA 1395.

On screen:
>Scenes from *El Karateca Azteca* [a Mexican B-movie from the '60s]

*Voiceover (**Cyber-Vato** speaking in a French intellectual accent):*
>It's working! Before the arrival of the Europeans in the New World, our ancestors' daily life was a perpetual ritual of dance, theater, music, poetry, and humor. There were no boundaries between life and performance. Even sports were performances. The Aztecs practiced a performative ball game which is the ancestor of squash, racketball, and football, but with a small difference: The team that lost had to be sacrificed to the gods. . . .

(back to live from studio)

El Naftazteca: My dilemma as a Mexican living in the United States is similar: if I lose, I die. Un paso en falso y me muero . . . norte sur, este o aquel. I don't forget that easy. *(close up: he eats a rubber heart)*

Letters appear on screen:

THEN THE CONQUISTADORES ARRIVED Y NOS LLEVO LA CHINGADA . . . SIN TRANSLATION

Scroll:

FIRST ENCOUNTERS/THE "CONQUISTA AU GO-GO" MUSIC VIDEO. CENTRAL MEXICO, CIRCA 1512. ARCHIVAL MATERIAL COURTESY OF "LA COMISIÓN ME CAGO EN EL QUINTO CENTENARIO."

Soundtrack:

"Amalia Batista" by *Los Xochimilcas*

On screen:

Conquist-au-Go-Go [Video excerpt of a performance in which Gómez-Peña as El Quebradito dances salsa with Miss Discovery '92 (Coco Fusco). Other dancing characters include a Spanish priest, a conquistador, and a tribe of "exotic primitives."]

Voiceover (Cyber-Vato using a French intellectual accent):

Historically speaking, Latino/Mexicano identity has been the product of an ongoing clash between the Indian, the European, and more recently, the gringo. . . . They are crucified by the four cardinal points, ruptured by myriad borders. . . . This permanent clash defines their sensibility, and is the raw material of their work.

(back to live from studio)

El Naftazteca: Hey you vatos, gimme a close-up with Camera One, and some special sound effects. *(he grabs a toy video camera)*

Amazing material, ¿que no? Performance . . . TV . . . identidad . . . contradicción . . . intervención pirata. For us — latino artists in the U.S., children of contradiction — identity has become the main subject of our art. We are obsessed with it . . . obsessed!! We play with it. We question it, expose it, subvert it, and push it to the limits, in hopes of developing more open and inclusive notions of the self. *(close-up, speaking directly to the camera)* Cruzo por lo tanto existes!

Cyber-Vato can be seen in the back of the TV studio, touching up his tattoo in a mirror.

El Naftazteca: From Aztec to high-tech, and everything in between, we contain many inner selves, and they constantly emerge on stage, often against our will. Check this out . . .

He speaks in tongues, puts on holographic glasses, and turns knobs on the control panel. The telephone rings. He answers several live phone calls.

Caller #1: *(very sincere)* Hi, this is Bill from Philadelphia. I just want to ask Naftaztec and Cyber-Vato if they have any recommendations for me. I'm going to Mexico for the first time and I want to know if I should go to Mazatlán or Cancun, and what should I wear? I want to do things right, I mean, respect the indios, and the whole thing.

El Naftazteca: Well, don't forget your Pepto-Bismol, carnal. *(to the camera)* Nice guy, eh?

(telephone rings)

Caller #2: Hey, this is Hank from Corpus Cristi. Listen, Naftaztec and Cyber-Vato, or whatever the hell you call yourselves, if you don't like it here, why don't you just go back where you came from? Huh? Vaya con dios, vatos locos. Hey, and remember the Alamo. *(gives a war whoop)*

El Naftazteca: Fax you, man!

(telephone rings again)

Caller #3: My name is Robert. I'm from Toronto. I'd just like to say that this program is a *really* good example of how primitive Third World countries are really capable of deconstructing the whole postmodern media paradigm.

El Naftazteca: Oh, thank you!

Caller #3: You know, we have a lot to learn from you. I just wish there was a larger Mexican community up here. The people of color up here just aren't as original.

El Naftazteca: Muchas gracias, carnalito. Estoy de acuerdo contigo. *(He holds up a "diablo" lotería card to the camera.)*

(telephone rings again)

Caller #4: Hey man, I'm from Montana. What do you guys do when you're not performing? You go back to jail or what? *(laughs)*

(El Naftazteca looks into his bone telephone, mimics the laughter, and hangs up. The telephone rings again.)

Caller #5: Actually, I'm in New York, close to where you are now. We have an important question to ask you: Why is this so Aztec-centric? Is Subcomandante Marcos in Chiapas an illegal alien? Okay, and what is the relationship between 187 and SOS?

(El Naftazteca answers each question in tongues. Telephone continues to ring.)

Caller #6: Hi, how are you? This is Ray from Lexington, Virginia, and I love your show. I just wanted to call in and tell you that I'm havin' a great time watchin' it and I was happy to hear you mention the Gulf War, 'cause I was there in the 101st Airborne and we kicked some ass! America, No. 1, right? Hooooooeeeeeeeey!!

(El Naftazteca doesn't answer and holds the "borracho" lotería card up to the camera, shaking his head.)

— END OF THE FIRST EXCERPT —

Letters fill the screen:

PART 5: "PERFORMANCE, TELEVISION, AND CYBER-SPACE"

El Naftazteca: *(live on screen, turns knobs and feeds chili peppers into a machine, speaking in a computerized voice)* So now, let's talk about the TECHNOPAL 2000, a technology originally invented by the Mayans with the help of aliens from Harvard. Its CPU is powered by Habañero chili peppers, combined with this or DAT technology, with a measured clock speed of 200,000 megahertz!

Cyber-Vato moves to center of studio and begins to move around like a New Age druggie.

El Naftazteca: *(continues to feed chilis into the TECHNOPAL while speaking)* It uses neural nets supplemented by actual chicken-brain matter and nacho cheese spread to supply the massive processing speed necessary for the machine to operate. And it's all integrated into one sombrero! Originally, the Chicano VR had to use a poncho, but with the VR sombrero, the weight is greatly reduced and its efficiency is magnified. And now, we have the first alpha version of the VR bandana dos mil, which Cyber-Vato will demonstrate for us!

Cyber-Vato wears a bandana over his eyes. It is connected by a rope to a robotic glove. Special effects on screen simulate the graphics and sounds of a virtual reality helmet.

El Naftazteca: What do you see, carnal?

Cyber-Vato: I'm in a car, driving down the road! No, somebody else is driving me.

El Naftazteca: What is he wearing?

Cyber-Vato: He's wearing a blue uniform and dark glasses. He seems like a cool guy.

El Naftazteca: Get his attention, tap him on the shoulder.

Cyber-Vato: I can't move my hands. *(scared)* They're handcuffed!!! Coño! That's a cop, take this pinche helmet off me!

El Naftazteca: Don't panic! Take control of the situation.

Cyber-Vato: He's coming at me with his nightstick!

El Naftazteca: Just get out of the car!

Cyber-Vato: But it's going really fast!

El Naftazteca: Don't worry, it's only virtual reality.

Cyber-Vato: *(breathing fast)* This is too real, ese! Change the program!!

El Naftazteca: Okay man, let me change the program. . . . You'll like this one. It's called "BorderScape 2000." *(graphics and music change to a New Age mood)* You are now in a beautiful meadow. It's sunset and the orange clouds are forming biblical scenes on the horizon. A cool breeze blows gently through your greasy hair.

Cyber-Vato: It's gorgeous, man! I feel happy, real happy.

El Naftazteca: What do you see?

Cyber-Vato: It's as if I was inside of a Southwest landscape painting. I see cactus, howling coyotes, magic all around me. The bushes are gently moving, as if they had a life of their own. Wait, a man is stepping out from behind a bush.

El Naftazteca: Who is he?

Cyber-Vato: It's, it's my UNCLE! Tio, what are you doing here? "Shut up, pendejo," he says. He points at a huge eagle flying above. A blinding light comes out of the eagle's beak. The vision is overwhelming. . . . *(his face is static)* It's a migra helicopter! The border patrol, ese. Tio, run, run! Delete, Naftazteca! *(completely panicking)* Change the program!!!

El Naftazteca: *(pressing a lot of buttons)* Okay, okay cobarde, you are now in America somewhere in the immediate future, you are Pete Wilson's undocumented gardener.
(His voice becomes a voiceover as an excerpt from the Mexican B-movie, El Hijo de la Calavera fills the screen: A Mexican charro confronts the owner of an hacienda with a gun, placing a human skull on his desk.)
You suddenly discover that Pito hired a gunman to kill the last gardener, so no one would find out he hired an illegal alien. You discover his skull in the garden, and now you're in Sacramento. You enter into Pito's office and confront him.

Letters flash on screen:

LIVE VR! DIRECT FROM TECHNOPAL

El Naftazteca: *(live on screen)* Remember . . . my name is El Naftazteca, end of the century disc-jockey. My friend here is El Cyber-Vato, and you lonesome güeros out there in TV-land are witnessing a historic pirate broadcast. Two intelligent, live Mexicans on national television. So . . . get off your nalgas pálidas and be interactive, carnales. Call the bunker right now and let us know what you think you think. Remember: You are allowed to speak in any language you wish. Illegal aliens are welcome. You are even allowed to be smart, performative, or poetic. Neta. *(the telephone rings)* Wow, another phone call. Así me gusta.

Phone Call: Are you the Naftazteca? . . . I think it's great what you are doing. But what I want to know is, who the hell are you really? I mean, are you legally in the U.S.? Do you have a green card? I mean, why do you have to be a pirate? Can't you just call a TV station and ask them to let you do your Shic-anou virtual reality stuff on normal prime-time TV? Can't you just do it legally? Don't you think you're contributing to the stereotype of the Mexican as a bandido?

El Naftazteca: *(speaking into his bone telephone)* Señorita, I'm sorry to disappoint you, but I don't have a green card, I changed it for the gold one. I appreciate your pertinent questions, but I want you to consider one remote possibility. Access to the media and access to high technology is not that easy, especially for people of color. Rarely do we get to be in control of our message, as we are now. Tonight at least, Cyber-Vato and I are in total control of the TV. We are controlling what you're seeing on national TV, perhaps for the very first time. Check out this video memory, jaina. *(turns knobs)*

Scroll:

IN 1985 GÓMEZ-PEÑA IS INVITED TO PERFORM FRAGMENTS OF HIS UPCOMING "OBRA DE TEATRO" AT A SPANISH-LANGUAGE CABLE STATION. INSTEAD, HE GETS CARRIED AWAY, DEVIATES FROM THE SCRIPT, AND TALKS ABOUT SEX, POLITICS, BORDER ISSUES, AND THE MEDIA.

On screen:

Footage from an early pirate TV intervention by Gómez-Peña.

*Voiceover (**El Naftazteca**):*

I remember my first guerrilla intervention in a TV station. It happened, I believe, in 1985, on a corny San Diego cable program. It was live, and I just couldn't help it. I didn't show the script to the director. He was in for a big surprise. Se cagó en los pantalones, el güey. He couldn't stop us. That was the first time I was put on a virtual blacklist.

(back to live from studio)

El Naftazteca: Well, enough is enough. You get the point. I'm sure you do. So now that you have experienced firsthand the amazing Chicano virtual reality machine, we've got some questions for you. So have a big sip of your beer or your milk shake, and put on your safety belt. Ready?

Cyber-Vato: Should performance art be allowed on national television? Call in and tell us yes or no, and why.

(telephone rings continuously)

El Naftazteca: Otra. Should people of color have more access to high technology? Can we handle high technology?

Cyber-Vato: Are you disgusted with what you have witnessed in the past hour? If so, tell us what exactly is causing your anger, the fact that I am Chicano, or the fact that I am being experimental, weird, and intellectually complex?

El Naftazteca: Perhaps the fact that I'm lying to you, since I'm not a TV pirate but a performance artist? . . . Should I give up and go back to Mexico?

Cyber-Vato: What if he can't go back?

El Naftazteca: What if he was born in Bakersfield or Utah? Come on, vatos, get off your nalgas pálidas. Call in and let us have it!

(telephone rings)

Phony call: My name is Prigone, the Mexican Vatican representative. What we are witnessing is the actual miracle of the birth of techno-religion. I proclaim you both to be the Holy Prophet Saints of Static!

Live on screen:

El Naftazteca and Cyber-Vato are standing in the studio with their arms in the air, as if they were being arrested. Suddenly, they are hit by gunshots. Static fills the screen. The telephone keeps on ringing as the sound of static grows louder, then a rock song by Los Dividos begins.

Preproduced segment:

El Naftazteca and Cyber-Vato stand and show their stigmatas through the static. They look like ghosts.

(The preproduced section slowly takes over the live image, until El Naftazteca and Cyber-Vato are transformed completely into static, becoming the Patron Saints of Static. The credits begin to roll.)

borderama

BORDERAMA

IN THE PRESS RELEASE FOR THIS PERFORMANCE, THE AUDIENCE IS invited: "Come to the show in costume, dressed as your favorite cultural other, ready to express those interracial fantasies we all have inside of us. Those who show up in costume will receive a special discounted ticket." Then they are warned: "This is not your average feelgood multi-culti piece."

Depending on the site, three to five local performance artists collaborate with us in advance, briefing us on important site-specific issues to incorporate into the ever-changing script, and helping to locate "special guests" (involuntary performance artists) from the community who are willing to participate in the experiment, even if their opinions differ from those of the artists. These "guests" might be local eccentrics, street performers, rappers, wrestlers, and/or local media celebrities. Their material is intertwined with the performance script. Since the final script is completed in collaboration with local artists, the actual performance ends up being substantially different at every site. An "ethnic fashion show" (not scripted), is staged by the entire collaborating team, and leads to an actual costume contest involving audience members at the end of the show.

The performance script has been developed through a series of residencies. During these residencies, we "test" the material in informal settings and workshops. We usually arrive one or two weeks before opening night, in order to work with the collaborating team toward the com-

Left: Typical intergenerational collaboration. Gómez-Peña and Roberto Sifuentes, Washington, D.C., 1995. Photo by Charles Steck

127

pletion of the script. Different versions of this performance, under different titles, have been performed in Los Angeles, San Francisco, Detroit, Denver, Boulder, New York, Helsinki, Washington, D.C., and Mexico City. The body of work is entitled the "Dangerous Border Game" series.

The "Dangerous Border Game" was written and directed in collaboration with Roberto Sifuentes and selected local voluntary and involuntary performance artists. The following version of the script does not include any of the material developed in collaboration with the local performers. It is still a work in progress as of this writing, December 1995.

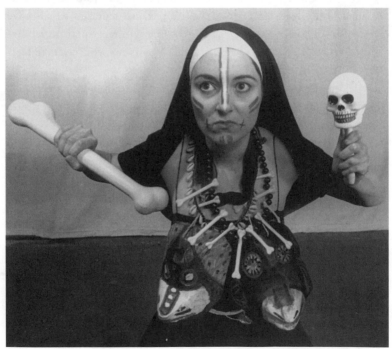

Poet Silvana Straw as an Afrophiliac nun in "Dangerous Border Game," at the Gala Hispanic Theater, Washington, D.C., 1995. Photo by Charles Steck

OPENING SCENE:

Note: The introductory sequence lasts approximately fifteen minutes, and changes dramatically from place to place.

As the audience enters the theater, a cellist dressed as a chola, or a naked Zapatista (with a black ski mask) plays European classical music onstage, while rap music by *Chicano to the Bone* (or Ry Cooder's military epic music) plays over the sound system. A fog machine periodically fills the space with smoke. A crucified skeleton hangs center stage. Five feathered, dead chickens hang from the ceiling at various heights, lit from different angles. A huge video screen projects "closed circuit" details of the performance and/or excerpts from *Naftaztec TV.*

A bottomless Zapatista (wearing a black ski mask) mops the stage in slow motion, while Gómez-Peña (wearing a straitjacket, a mariachi hat, boxer shorts, and snakeskin Norteño boots) is paraded around the stage in a wheelchair by a "tourist" (wearing a tropical dress & a blond wig, carrying a camera). He is eventually positioned center stage. The Zapatista stands behind him, holding the mop as though it were a weapon.

The tourist kneels in front of GP, giving him head, while he sings "Besame Mucho," his voice filtered to sound satanic. Once the tourist is finished, she stands up and gives a fascist salute.

Sifuentes (wearing a three-piece suit) fumigates the space in a ritual manner with a DDT spray gun. Once the audience is seated, he stands behind a lectern (stage left) and freezes. The music fades out.

PART I: IDENTITY ESCAPE ACT

The tourist handles a "closed circuit" video camera, capturing facial expressions of RS & GP, as well as details from the set, which are played on a screen hanging from the ceiling behind the performers.

129

RS/(AUTHORITARIAN TONE):

A mariachi in a straitjacket? Naked Zapatistas and Las Vegas shamans? A (description of musician) performing (name of the composer) to rap music, and dead chickens, all at (name of the space, and city)? This is the end of the world . . . as we know it. Gómez-Peña, stand up, walk towards the audience, walk!! *(GP gets up and tries to walk, but falls on his face. The Zapatista helps him up.)* Walk! *(GP finally gets to center stage. The two other performers leave the stage.)* Now, show your face! . . . *(to the audience).* Look at this guy. He was a MacArthur fellow, official iconoclast, published author and shit . . .

MUSIC BEGINS: ALBINIONI'S "ADAGGIO" BY GERMAN GROUP *EXCEPTION*

RS/LOUDLY, EVANGELIST VOICE (INTO MEGAPHONE):
But now, raza,
you are about to witness a miracle on stage
an identity escape act never before presented to a live audience
a Hispanic who, having lost his way to Aztlán,
will experience a conversion right here, on stage
& will find his inner indio,
the tiny indio we all have inside of us,
trapped in a 500-year-old inner prison,
the gringo prison within.
So, Gómez-Peña, go for it & please do not divert from the script.

GP/REVIVAL-STYLE CONFESSIONAL VOICE (FILTERED BY SPX MACHINE):
Queridos compañeros Aztlanecas
tonight, I must confess. . . . I . . . have . . . sinned . . .
Yes, I have been a sinner in my private life
a politically incorrect mother-fucker taco boy
I beg you to excuse my direct language
but I've been told by my therapist to let it all out tonight.

Right on William, aviéntate!

I hope you understand, my dear razza

rrazza!

digo rraza!
that my sins are a product of my own internalized colonialism
my own self-hatred produced by working for ten years
in the heart of the U.S. art world.

Say it, bro!

I didn't choose to be accepted, but that's beside the point.
The fact is that I was, & I am a sinner, un pecador de aquellas!!
A brown decadent culero sinner . . .

(interrupting) **Brother, get to the point!**

Tonight I must confess to all of you that . . .

Say it, cabron!

I, I, I have desired white women . . . quite often
even now, at this very moment as I talk to you
I am dying to go to bed with a blond German anthropologist
with freckles on her pink breasts.

Stand up tall, and face us!!

I'm sorry but *(breathing)* I'm having an erection as I speak.

Halleluja!

I know, I am a sexist apolitical vendido hijo de su pinche . . .
& the Chicana goddesses out there
you all have the divine right to whip me
(screaming) right now!

Stop the music maestro!

Sisters, please come onstage.
Strip the guilt from this carnalito & whip him! Sabrosso!

RS goes into the audience and finds a female volunteer to whip GP.

Whip me for Tezcatlipoca's sake!!

Should she do it? *(3 times)*

With the audience encouraging her, she whips him several times.

Ay!! Ayy!! Que rrico, harder!

MUSIC RESUMES.

Calm down & continue, pecador.

But my sins go beyond my sexual life
my favorite film director is . . .

Say it!

Wim Wenders, not Robert Rodriguez.

Ay!!

Yes, I prefer Rage Against the Machine to Banda Machos
yes, I prefer Annie Sprinkle to Rubén Martinez.
What's wrong with me?

What's wrong with him?

I act as if I had been born in Pasadena or New Jersey
to a dysfunctional Anglo family.

What's wrong with you?

You are always pretending to be something you are not.
Accept it, bro! You're just a Taco Bell performance artist,
an abortion of Telemundo . . .

Yes, I pretend, I pretend to be an implacable nacionalista in public,
"El Warrior for Gringostroika" & shit. . . .

Spit it out, pollo loco!

It's pitiful, I don't deserve to be listened to anymore.
Don't listen to me, carnales!!

**Come on, Yiguermo, Guiliermou, be more specific
& tell them how have you betrayed the indio in you.**

I . . . I have . . . I have been to McDonalds twice in the past six months
I had a McFajita with ketchup picante . . .
& I didn't vomit.
I tried but . . . it just didn't come out.
I know, I'm a gringolatra, it's a disease raza!!
I just can't control it.
I even forgot the lyrics of "La Cucaracha"
& worst of all, & worst of all . . .

Spit it out! They'll understand.

I didn't attend the last Day of the Dead . . .

Ay!!

& you know fuckin' why?

Why, ese?

I signed up for a Halloween piercing seminar instead.
Yes, my genitals are pierced, tattooed.
At least I have a pre-Columbian tattoo . . .

Halleluja!

Well, half pre-Columbian:
a Bart Simpson riding on a flaming Quetzalcoatl.
It's cool, chido,
but its not like I had it done in la pinta.

Halleluja! *(twice)*

So next morning,
I woke up feeling like nacho-cheese spread.
It felt like my identity had melted for good
& I knew I had to change.
I mean, pretending to be some kind of spokesperson for la razzza . . .

rraza güey!
rraza power, everybody!

(GP breaks out in tears.) and I'm not even a Chicano
you know, I was born in Mexico.
I am very sorry, but I didn't choose to be born in Mexico.
It was my parents' mistake.
(crying)
I am nothing *(twice)*

He is nothing! *(twice)*

but a Chicano impersonator
world-beat Indian
multicultural Frankenstein
walking Mexican curio
by-product of NAFTA
gringo-lover, cappuccino-monger,
veggie burrito, a chorizo on a croissant!!
And on top of that

Say it!

and on top of that,
my accent is fake!!

(pause)
I don't really talk like this at home, but that's peripheral,
I mean, everything about me is peripheral.

Listen to the ancient pain of this carnalito!

So do me a favor & shoot me!
Take this unbearable pain away from me
& let me go to gringo hell, once & for all.

GP falls down and contorts as if possessed. He shakes off his straitjacket to reveal an Aztec chest piece underneath.

Come on, raza . . .
he is already in gringo hell without even realizing it.
He needs all your political support.
Raza, say you forgive him.
Come on, we forgive you Yermo, Guermo, Yiguermo.
Tell him, vato, it's okay to be confused.
We are all phony Chicano impersonators
& only the Virgen de Guadalupe up there
can show us the one & only way to Aztlán.
Come on Lupita, this suffering soul needs your redemption!
Everybody, come on, join hands & help us . . .
heal this confused carnal, heal him!

Audience joins in: "Heal him, heal him . . ."

MUSIC ENDS.

RS picks GP up, puts a feathered Aztec headdress on him, and orders him to speak in Náhuatl: "Gómez-Peña, speak in Náhuatl!" GP raises his fist in a fascist salute and speaks a few phrases in pseudo-Náhuatl. Then RS gives *him a plastic trumpet and orders him: "**Now, play!**" GP plays a sad Mexican waltz. RS tells the audience to clap along: "**Everybody!**" Prerecorded screams interrupt the action.*

MUSIC: "LOS HIJOS DE LA CHINGADA" BY MEXICAN ROCK GROUP *BOTELLITA DE JEREZ*

SLOW FADE TO TOTAL BLACKOUT.

During blackout, GP puts on a fake zebra-skin tuxedo jacket and Stetson hat, grabs a rubber heart and toy accordion and sits in the wheelchair. RS stands behind lectern.

PART II: LA NOSTALGIA
(The Existentialist Mojado & the Hypnotist)

GP plays a tiny Tex-Mex accordion in the wheelchair. In the background, the Zapatista mops the stage in slow motion. Lights come up.

RS/NARRATIVE VOICE:

In these times of acute emotional pain and political confusion, we often find refuge in nostalgia, but sometimes even nostalgia is hard to find, and that's why *you* go to the therapist, but *we* can't afford a therapist. And since he doesn't even speak Spanish, our pain doesn't translate, so we end up visiting the hypnotist at the local barrio lounge. But that ends up being a dangerous experience, since nostalgia, as we all know, distorts identity.

RS puts on cheap-looking silver turban and 3-D glasses and holds up a dead chicken, swinging it like a pendulum. A laser beam hits the chicken's head. RS orders GP to stop playing the accordian.

RS: Shut up, Quebradito! And, pick up your script, man. You are always forgetting your lines.

RS/HYPNOTIST VOICE(COMPUTER-ALTERED):
Everyone take a deep breath, in . . . out . . .
Now, with your right hand reach over and grab the crotch of your
neighbor.
Massage . . . Gently . . .
Relax, reeeelax.
*(GP does relax asanas in the wheelchair, and is racked by convulsions during
parts of the following text.)*
You are very stressed out and drunk with confusion.
It was a hard year, ¿que no?
The L.A. quake, the Zapatista insurrection,
the passage of NAFTA, the assassination of Colosio,
the collapse of the alternative art world,
the death of Frank Zappa & Jackie O,
SOS, Prop. 187, the devaluation of the peso . . .
Ay! too much weight on the wet back of one little Mexican.
Stop moving, carajo!
Remember . . . you are not responsible
so close your eyes & breathe deeply . . .
Now, slowly go back to your earliest memories
(GP speaks in tongues.)
cross the border in reverse
retrace the footprints of your migration
remember each and every trauma.
We'll use the Mexican method, la nostalgia . . .
so, take a drink & listen to your favorite tune.

GP pulls rubber heart from his crotch and drinks from it.

MUSIC BEGINS: MEXICAN BLUES

RS: *(counts down)* 10, 9, 8, 7, 6, 5, 4, 3, 2, 1

GP/MUY SENTIMENTAL:
Ay, la nostalgia
la nostalgie, yeah, yeah, wow, wow
protects me against the gringos, la migra, the art world. . . .
Qué fuckin' chingón pasado I had.
My past, pasado, pasadíssimo . . .
el esss . . . mog que me vió crecer,
las chavas de la banda, jariosas, tiernísimas . . .

Please, can you remember in English?

Where is the interpreter we asked for?
Where is the consulate flota when we need them?

Tranquilo, sultán. This is not a binational summit.

(to the chicken) See pollito, we are alone, en inglés, in this gringo world.

Don't be so epiphanic, man. Tell me about the departure.

The departure, la partida man, qué partida de maaadres!
My mamita man,
my land cut in half with a gigantic blade, gachíiiisimo!!
We live, therefore we cross

I follow you, mojado.

the journey tu sabes, siempre hacia el Norte.

El Norte?

I mean my North, my-gration, my dangerous poetry
la pinche journey within
Tijuana, la Revu, la placa, los coyotes *(howls)*
la migra man, their guns guapa, los dogos infernales *(barks)*
to' mordido bro
like you, llegué to' mordido y mojado a California
wet back, wet feet, wet dreams, that's me
they call me "Supermojado" . . .

So now that you are on this side, what do you feel?

Fear, man, un culture shock de aquellas.
Los skinheads, bikers, cristianos y demás patriotic Califeños,
those vatos give me the creeps.

Where are you?

Mickey, Mikiztli, Califas, the House of the Dead
San Diego, Los Angeles, Fresno, I'm not quite sure . . .

Give me some images, feelings . . . go . . .

Images, tiny angels scattered all over the pavement
sirens . . . spotlights . . . surrounded by cops, man.
Busted seven times, myself apañadísimo
for looking like this
for looking "suspicious"
hiper-Mexican enchilado
el Go-Mex siempre horny, scared and intersticial
filled with all these ancestral memories, ancestral memories . . .

Give me those memories.
(GP speaks in tongues.)
No, that's too far back.
Something more juicy & topical macho.

Conversations y entrepiernas on the beach,
el agua fría y contaminada.
"Ti quierrou my King Tacou Marriachio
tu poner tu chili con carñi dentrou dee my tostada shell."
"I lav yu jani babe, nalguita descolorida."
(he seems happy & horny) California fornicare sin memoria.

That's juicy, macho. Give me more details.

Earthquakes, fire, riots, gunshots in the distance

more

the end of Western civilization

more

the end of a million Mexican journeys

and then . . .

and then . . . I hit the road again.
(melancholy) Northeast this time,
through Phoenix, Denver, Detroit,
the Big Smoke, Bigg Sssmoke,
Chicago, si . . . cago . . . in Spanish still
(acts as if he's shitting) ca-gan-do sobre la costra cultural de Gringolandia.

Coño! Speak in English, pinche wetback!

Sin translation pues, sin papers digo, to role, to lick, to write . . .

Continue walking man, where are you now?

I think I am in (name of city)
(sings) "Stop singing the blues . . ."

What blues, man? Be more specific.

RS's voice effect off. Delay effect on both voices; GP speeds up his delivery.

I mean, what to make of all these loqueras?
I feel a bit confucio & lonesome tonight.
Where are my dear friends?
(screams the names of several close friends)
Are you vatos still alive?
Are your minds and hearts still intact?

Yo estoy aqui muriéndome en (name of city)
America, ca, ca, ca-put, digital mortis
la gran soledad de los United
pero bien united . . . de los cojones, I mean . . .

You are losing me, carnal.

(screaming) estamos united, ¿que no?
unidos por el temor y la soledad

You are losing your audience, Gómez-Peña . . .
These poor people don't speak Spanglish.

Absolutely lonely es bien Ameerrican. They know!

You are using language to hide, to avoid the issue, culero!

(GP drinks some more from the rubber heart.)
Qué issue, man?
Que tiempos nos han tocado vivir.
Que western utopia ni que la chingada
(with a French accent)
chingada-da-da, da-da
les enfantes de la chingada
dans la grand topographie de fin de siecle, ¡ay güey!

Voice effect off. GP takes off his hat and dark glasses.

Enough pathos, Baudelaire,
and please, drop the script.
It's getting real corny.
(to sound technician) **Hey, give me effect #70 . . .**
(computerized voice effect back on RS) **That's it!**
Now, Gómez-Peña, slowly come back.
I'm holding your hand,
your soul, your fragile identity . . .

RS counts down from 10 to 1, intertwined with GP's following text.

I wake up many years later
with my friend Roberto onstage
in a country at war
in a city at war
in a neighborhood at war
in an institution at war.
My audience is composed
of victims of political torture
but they don't know it
they don't remember
they don't want to remember . . .
I mean, who wants to remember nowadays?

Not me, man.

Music fades out. Laser beam goes out.

BLACKOUT.

GP changes into "Las Vegas Shaman" costume: leopard-skin mask, tiger-skin vest, and holding a wooden snake. Bare-chested Zapatista turns into "Zapatista dominatrix."

PART III: AN EXCERSISE IN REVERSED ANTHROPOLOGY

RS goes to lectern, puts on a "French intellectual" mask, and grabs a laser pointer. Slides begin.

SLIDE #1: FRENCH COMIC HERO *FANTOMAS* BEING ATTACKED BY MEXICAN SHAMANS

RS/FRENCH ANTHROPOLOGIST(HEAVY FRENCH ACCENT):
    Bon soir rrazza. Bienvenue a esta mamada. As you have seen so farr, Mexicans are obsessed with memory. Such a paradox: A Mexican

speaking bad English, and a Chicano speaking awful Spanish, two confused generations onstage, in search of an impossible bridge, an original
image, a glimpse of hope . . . c'est dommage! But since you have no previous references for Mexican culture, I will introduce you to some basic
data. During my recent trip to dangereuse Mexique, I collected a series
of images and indigenous sounds, reflective of the contemporary yet
ancient spirit of that marvelously confused society.

MUSIC BEGINS: MEXICAN STREET MUSIC MIXED WITH BARKING DOGS

SLIDE #2: TACOSAURUS

RS: Way before the first Americans
migrated from Siberia via the Bering
Strait, there were already Mexican
creatures roaming around this savage
continent. Voici we see an edible
sample of these specimens. Contrary
to perceptual illusion, Tacosaurus
was . . . this big. *(signals size between thumb and forefinger)*

SLIDE #3: SCENE FROM A PSEUDO-AZTEC CODEX (TWO PRIESTS SACRIFICING A BLOND TOURIST)

RS: Since the earliest encounters with the civilized West, as we can see
in this pictograph from an early Aztec codex, Mexicans have always
exhibited hostility towards well-meaning missionaries, anthropologists,
curators, and tourists. This performance is but one bad example . . .

SLIDE #4: SCENE OF HERNAN CORTEZ & LA MALINCHE ABOUT TO HAVE SEX

RS: Yet, Mexicans clearly understand the power of erotic seduction.
Here, in this archival photo, we see the original bilingual secretary of
the Americas, La Malinche, about to engage *(sinister laughter)* in the very
first indigenous contact with Europe. Cortez didn't know what he was

143

getting into . . . the creation of an entire new race! Les enfants de la chingada . . .

SLIDE #5: AZTEC WARRIOR POPO & PRINCESS IXTA VACATIONING AT MONTEZUMA'S NATIONAL PARK

RS: Effectivement, since pre-Columbian times, Mexicans have always been migratory creatures. In this rare photo we see Aztec warrior Popocatépetl and his fiancée Princess Ixtaccíhuatl vacationing at a popular U.S. amusement park in the early 1400s.

SLIDE #6: THE POPE SAYS MASS FOR A GROUP OF CHAMULA INDIANS FROM CHIAPAS

GP & Zapatista dominatrix adopt positions on stage. He sits on a chair center stage and begins to tame a wooden snake while speaking in tongues. Zapatista dominatrix does stylized S&M fashion poses, stage right.

RS: Although they claim to be Christian, indios are usually pagan. Voici Pope John Paul tries to talk a group of lascivious indios out of practicing safe sex, performance art, and idolatry. *(excited)* By the way, I have a special treat for you tonight. I have brought from the southeast Mexican rain forest two real live specimens: an authentic Mexican shaman *(lights on GP)* and a real live exotic revolutionary *(lights on dominatrix)* who will illustrate eloquently my point. If we could have a little applause from the audience to make them feel welcome. . . . Thank you. And the Benetton photographers may now approach the stage to take pictures. . . . Aren't they mignon, colorful?

SLIDE #7: PROMO PHOTO OF FLAMBOYANT MEXICAN WRESTLING TEAM

RS: Following the examples of the European communité and the Pacific Rim, our three North American neighbors decided to sign a Free Trade Agreement, a sort of Ménage à Trade. Mexico provides raw material, talent, and manpower; Canada, the technologie; and the U.S. is the sole recipient of the goodies. Smart, n'est-ce pas? Here, you can enjoy the official promo photo of the NAFTA Negotiating Team.

SLIDE #8: CLOSE-UP OF THE BLEEDING FACE OF A MEXICAN WRESTLER

RS: Whoops! One of the first casualties of NAFTA. Next image, please.

SLIDE #9: FIVE ELDERLY ZAPATISTAS POSING WITH THEIR WEAPONS

RS: Diorama of angry Zapatistas at the Musée of Natural History. Sadly, Mexicans can't handle modernity, so when the country was finally on the verge of joining the First World under the leadership of President Pedillo, a group of dilettante foreign saboteurs disguised as indios took up arms following the ancient spirit of "Zapato."

SLIDE #10: BEER ADVERTISEMENT DEPICTING TWO BLOND MODELS DRESSED AS MEXICAN REVOLUTION-ARIES

RS: Next ethnographic diorama: typical Zapatista adelitas; les demoiselles du Chiapas.

SLIDE #11: PERFORMANCE SHOT OF GÓMEZ-PEÑA & SIFUENTES AS BORDER MAFIOSI

RS: The East L.A. cartel, better known as "La Pocha Nostra." Here, captured in a rare photo, we see the two alleged art dealers and well-known narco-satanic mafiosi: Gómez-Peña, alias "El Quebradito," et Sifuentes, otherwise known as "Cyber-Vato."

SLIDE #12: TWO MEXICAN WRESTLERS IN PINK ATTIRE.

RS: Ici, we see them during a special mission traveling incognito in traditional Mexican attire. The duo often mask their seditious political agenda as performance art. In cahoots with members of other cartels, these cultural terrorists are committed to the destruction of our western value systems and sacred institutions, like this one.

SLIDE #13: THREE MIDGET BULLFIGHTERS

RS: Tijuana mini-bullfighters. Don't let their size and exotic costumes deceive you. They are petite, but powerful and mean-spirited. They have control over all the street vendors of Los Angeles and all the coyotes who smuggle Mexicans across the border.

SLIDE #14: FEMALE WRESTLER

RS: Implacable Chicana feminist leader "La Licuadora." She pulverizes her enemies in the macho Chicano nationalist cartel, therefore she has a bittersweet relationship with Gómez-Peña and Sifuentes, who often present to their audiences questionable images of women, for example . . . *(pause)*

SLIDE #15: FEMALE BIKER WITH HER TORSO COMPLETELY COVERED WITH TATTOOS

RS: But her main rival is an urban primitive performance artist named "Lola Biker," the lover of Cyber-Vato. She leads a movement to reclaim the body as a site for pleasure and pain in the apocalyptic society of the end of the century.

The lights on GP & Zapatista dominatrix go out. GP stands up, takes his chair offstage, and waits for RS to finish lecture. Dominatrix leaves the stage.

SLIDE #16: SKINHEAD WRESTLER

RS: Il y a Monsieur Harold Ezell, the bodyguard of California governor Pito Wilson and head of anti-immigrant narco-citizen group "esse o esse." Their objective is to deport all Mexicans back to Los Angeles and San Antonio. Notre temps sont trop bizarres, ¿que no?

SLIDE #17: NAFTA EMBLEM

RS: Now, as we enter the 21st century, let's see what self-proclaimed radical performance artists are doing. . . . *(pause)* And now, madams & monsieurs, directly from the capital of the American crisis, Cyber-Vato and El Charromántico, performing an enigmatic, yet macabre, cyber-punk techno-nationalist ethno-ritual for disenfranchised Anglo minorities in search of truth and leadership.

BLACKOUT.

PART IV: RITUAL TRANSFORMATION IN THE TRADITIONAL CHICANO BUTOH STYLE

RS moves to center stage. Stagehands bring a small table and chair. On the table is a pair of handcuffs, a bandana, and a leather strap. GP changes into a mariachi costume offstage. Lights come up.

MUSIC: "SOUTH OF THE BORDER"

A close-up of RS taken by closed circuit video is shown on a screen hanging from the ceiling as he performs the following actions: He takes off his suit in slow motion to reveal a "holy gang member" costume underneath — a muscle T-shirt, riddled with bullet holes and stained with blood. He slowly puts on a bandana headband, dark glasses, and the handcuffs, while a hanging chicken descends from the ceiling on a rope. He wraps the leather strap around his face.

At the end of this "ritual transformation," GP — now dressed as a mariachi — stands behind the lectern and freezes. Lights on GP, who begins to sing "Hotel California" with his voice altered by the SPX machine to sound satanic. He then begins a talk on censorship and language, but the sound system keeps shutting off during his delivery, as if he is being censored.

BLACKOUT.

RS grabs a police baton and delivers the following text. GP puts on a mariachi hat and remains behind the lectern.

RS: NAFTA has been good . . . to us. The Trinational Arts Commission has hired many Latino performance artists to promote art as a safe investment . . . like this evening, for example. Guillermo & I are currently working on a TV commercial, and we want to share it with you. So first . . . imagine over there a live band of naked mariachis, a lowrider car right here, and thirty Frida Kahlo look-alikes of all shapes, sizes & colors, male & female, dancing bien sexy. So, is everyone ready on the set? Tape #5 rolling . . .

RS fumigates the hanging chicken, then pulls the bandana down over his eyes, adopts the position of hitting a piñata, and freezes. The Zapatista and the tourist adopt a praying position under a hanging chicken, stage left. The Zapatista dips her hand into a bowl of blood and slowly wipes it on her bare chest, while the tourist burns incense.

PART V: FREE-TRADE ART PIÑATA PARTY

Portions of GP's text for this section are prerecorded, and repeated live by GP with his voice filtered in various ways. While GP delivers the following text, RS tries to hit the "chicken piñata" with the police baton, but misses over and over. Lights on GP.

GP: Cameras, one, two, rolling down your psyche
Ay Mexico, rrrromantic Mexico
Musica maestro! Musica!!
Pues nos la echamos sin música . . .

TAPE BEGINS: PRERECORDED TEXT

RS begins trying to hit the chicken, reminding GP of his lines when he "forgets" them.

GP/MEROLICO VOICE (MOUTHING OR SPEAKING ALONG WITH THE TAPE AT A DIFFERENT RHYTHM):
Bienvenidos a Naftalandia
damas y caballeros
lovers/consumers of Pura Bi-cultura.
A new transcontinental breeze ricochets
from Monterrey to Manhattan
from D.F. to L.A. and beyond
we perceive the pungent smells
of chili con ketchup & diet mole.
Never before had Gringolandia
DON FRANCISCO VOICE:
digo, America . . . succumbed
to the sabor of "the Amigo Country"
with such eagerness & gusto
(he forgets his lines for a second)
. . . qué sigue, mister?

. . . oh yes, the Frida shit. . . .
Let Frida Kahlo's monkeys run wild in your dreams
get lost in the labyrinth of solitude of a Mexican painting
dance yourself to sleep with the sounds of quebradita
don't forget to wear your conceptual sombrero, güerita
enjoy the spicy nipples of a ranchero diva
the feathered genitalia of a transvestite Matachin.
Go for it! Uno is not enough.
Don't arrive late to the grand tri-national fi-es-ta
MEROLICO VOICE:
su-support NAFTArt
Free Trade Art for the clepto-Mexican connoiseur.
Join a new vibrant gastro . . . erotic . . . econo . . .
cu-cultural ma-ma-quiladora
y de paso contribute to 187 . . .
(speaking very fast)
You'll receive a 200-page catalog
certified by Televisa & the Metropolitan.
You can place your orders de volada
by simply dialing your resident alien number
or by speaking directly to our representative after the show.
DON FRANCISCO VOICE:
Ajjuuua! No one can like a Mexi-can.
No one knows like those Chicanous.
Approach your funders de ya
porque Free Raid . . . ssshhit!
That was a typo, ese. *(he appears embarrassed and apologetic)*

RS: *(still swinging at the chicken)* Come on, you're fuckin' up. I'm coming after you next!

GP folds his hands as if praying or begging.

GP/COOL BUT DESPERATE & APOLOGETIC:
I'm sorry, I didn't mean to . . .
I'm having an identity crisis on stage
I don't know what I'm saying
la neta es que . . . I need a job real bad!
The art spaces don't want to invite us anymore
you know, identity politics are dead
Mexicans are on the hit list
(screams)
DRUNKEN NORTEÑO VOICE (WITH DELAY):
Can anyone give me a job?
(uncomfortable pause)
Don't you guys practice affirmative action & relocation?
Pues rrrelocate me right now
que estoy rreloco
before you re-pa-triate my bones to Hollywood
or to the Smithsonian
MEROLICO VOICE (STOP DELAY):
(speaking very fast)
I can cook, clean, translate, guide tours in Náhuatl & Arawak,
maqui-le-hago lo que quiera
gardening, security, community outreach, Aztec massage
got my resident alien card barata
my social security number is 001-42-819
(he pauses and breathes deeply)
NORMAL VOICE:
Wait, I got an idea, man.
Roberto, find an interesting tableau & freeze.

RS pulls out a knife and decapitates the hanging chicken, dropping its body to the floor. He adopts a "crucified" position, with his arms draped over the police baton.

GP: Are there any museum people here?
Anyone from the Museum of Tolerance, perhaps?
Would you accept us as part of your permanent collection?
A living, dying, authentic Mexican diorama,
or would you rather see more action: Okay,
Roberto, adopt a better tableau and freeze.
Scene four, zero tolerance, action!

Lights off GP. Spotlight on RS. Tape stops.

Naked Zapatista cellist begins to play a melancholy tune. RS starts beating the chicken with the police baton. He beats the hell out of it; this goes on for as long as it takes for him to completely smash the chicken to bits, and he is breathing hard and sweating with the effort after a while. When it is finally completely destroyed, he collapses onto his knees. He gathers the chicken's remains into a pile, then picks it up and holds it in a romantic, almost erotic posture. While he does this, GP grabs a huge knife and walks toward him. As GP steps into RS's spotlight, taped music begins to play.

MUSIC BEGINS: "STAND BY ME"

GP takes off the mariachi hat and places it on RS's head. He raises the knife over his head and brings it down to stab RS in slow motion saying, "Chick, chicken, Chicano . . . Power!"

BLACKOUT.

FINALE: "FREE TRADE SEX AUCTION"

GP & RS grab two chairs and sit on the edge of the stage, with their heads covered by brown paper bags. Lights on them. The Zapatista and the tourist begin to strike the show.

TAPE BEGINS: PRERECORDED FEMALE VOICE (FINNISH ACCENT):

Well, well, the performance is finally over. Now, would anyone like to spend the night with two sexy AIDS-free Third World performance artists for only 25 pesos? Free Trade Sex, the ultimate border experience. Please, feel free to walk onstage & touch the performance artists, lick them, smell them, massage them, but don't go too far unless you are willing to pay the piper. The Mexican male on the right weighs 75 kilos, sings Italian opera & loves German cinema. Although still undocumented, he has been blessed by the Whitney Biennial. The younger Chicano on the left plays soccer with Central American refugees, speaks French & makes a mean enchilada. The April issue of *Play Chola* has named him "The Chuco Hefner" of '95. They are not trained actors, mind you, but they have great imagination and charisma. Remember, the only true means toward intercultural communication in the '90s is sex. It's only 25 pesos, barato, so don't be culeros.

(ten seconds of silence)

MUSIC BEGINS: "CAMELIA LA TEJANA" BY *LA LUPITA*

The loud music breaks the dramatic tension. Audience begins to applaud. The performers stand up and take the bags off their heads. Optional: The ethnic fashion show begins.

— AND THE SHOW GOES ON —

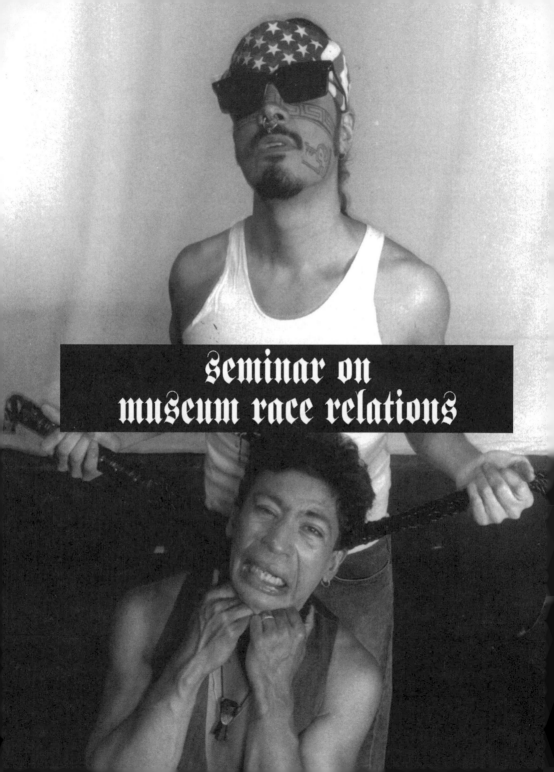

seminar on
museum race relations

A SEMINAR ON MUSEUM RACE RELATIONS

The space is lit like a TV studio. Gómez-Peña and Sifuentes are dressed as sleazy motivational seminar instructors, wearing three-piece suits in the colors of the Mexican flag. Occasionally, GP walks through the aisles and onto the runway with a handheld maraca microphone. RS remains behind a lectern most of the time. Key moments are punctated by tropical muzak and lights.

RS: Let's conduct a little experiment to loosen up a bit. Would you please all stand up, reach for your neighbor's hand, close your eyes, and breathe in, breathe out, breathe in, breathe out. . . . *(the audience obeys, GP joins in)*

MUSIC BEGINS: "I WANT TO LIVE IN AMERICA" BY *THE TIJUANA BRASS*

GP & RS dance a tropical twist on the runway.

GP: Hello, my name is Bill.

RS: And I'm Bob.

GP: Welcome (name of city), to the seminar on museum race relations, developed by Smithsonian experts. You don't need to know anything about art to be here, but there is one condition: you must be sincere. All we ask from you is to open your wounded hearts and answer everything we ask. Our only objective is to help you overcome those involuntary racist tendencies, those colonial traumas you have unjustly inherited . . .

Left: Chicano/Salvadoreño relations in the '90s. Roberto Sifuentes and Quique Aviles, Washington, D.C., 1995. Photo by Charles Steck

RS: There will be two kinds of questions. Some directed to certain participants, and others to be answered by whoever wishes to do so. It will all make sense at the end. So this is your last chance . . . those who don't wish to play may leave the theater now. . . . No one? This is America!

GP: First, we need some basic information from you. How many Latinos are there in the audience? Please raise your hands. *(he counts them)* You, sir . . . do you wish to be called "Mexican," "Latino," "Hispanic," "greaser," or something else? Why? *(the man answers)* Thanks for your sincerity.

RS: What about Native Americans? Is anyone 1/64-th Cherokee? *(he counts them)* You, sir . . . do you know which Nation you are from? Are you registered? Thanks for your sincerity. Isn't America great?

GP: How many bi- or trilingual people do we have here? *(he counts)* Órale not bad for (name of city)! Señorita, can you please curse in the other language you know? *(she obeys)* Thank you. And you, sir? Woooooow!

RS: Let's all curse in other languages at the top of our lungs. Ready? 1 . . . 2 . . . 3 . . . *(everybody screams)* Makes you feel good, ¿que no?

MUSIC FADES OUT.

GP: Liberating. . . . Now it's time to enter a deeper level of cross-cultural com-mu-ni-ca-tion. Repeat after me: cross-cultural com-mu-ni-ca-tion. Beautiful! Now, those who think they are definitely not racists, can you please raise your hands? Sir, can you explain why you raised your hand? *(he answers)* Is everyone satisfied with his answer? *(if not)* Why not?

RS: By a show of hands, how many of you in the last month have experienced racism? How about sexism? Homophobia? How about police harassment? Would anyone like to share that incident? *(someone volunteers)*

GP: Heavy. . . . We are rolling! See how easy it is to trust other human beings? How many of you have hired illegal domestic help? To the lady over there, from which nationality ma'am? *(she answers)* Did you feel guilty for doing it? Thanks again for your sincerity. This is America!

RS: Are we having fun yet? Isn't this cathartic? How many of you think that immigrants are definitely contributing to America's downfall? Can anyone answer why?

GP: How many of you voted for Proposition 187? *(if someone admits to it)* Can anyone show this man out the door? Now, how many of you think the U.S./Mexico border should be opened? I need three good reasons. *(someone answers)* One . . . *(someone else answers)* Two . . . Three? . . .

(Often at this point people in the audience begin to shyly debate with one another, but we cut them off.)

RS: How many of you think that political correctness has gone too far? Be careful what you say! You never know who is out there. *(someone answers)* Can you please elaborate more, sir?

GP: How many of you feel that as artists we have no business asking all these heavy questions? *(someone answers)*

RS: Do you feel that art must only entertain, decorate your home, or create positive images of an oppressed culture? *(if no one answers, he asks energetically)* What do you think about the future of the NEA? *(if no one answers)* Do you think anything at all?

GP: Now that we are all really close to one another, let's get into the third level of *(GP & RS together)* cross-cul-tu-ral com-mu-ni-ca-tion: dark secrets. Please, close your eyes again, take a deep breath and grab your neighbor's crotch. Yeah. . . . Are there any people in the audience who secretly fantasize about being from a different race or nationality? *(RS delivers his next text, overlapping with GP as he continues)* Come on, I always wanted to be Croatian myself. Sir, which race would you like to be? And you, ma'am?

RS: *(simultaneously)* Indian . . . Latino . . . Arab . . . African American . . . Carajo! No audience participation?

GP: Please raise your hands, those of you Anglo-Americans who have had sex with a person of color or an "illegal alien" in the last month. *(several do)* Would anyone like to describe that incident? *(if no one goes for it)* Puritans . . .

RS: Okay. It's our turn to let it all hang out. Everything you ever wanted to know about Chicanos and Mexicans, but were too shy or afraid to ask, you may ask us now!

(Three plants in the audience begin to ask some questions. Audience members may ask other things, and we must ad-lib.)

Plant #1: To the Mexican: Is it true that Latins are good lovers?
GP: *(answers in tongues, or says yes but shakes head no)*

Plant #2: To the Chicano guy: What's a Chicano?
RS: An American impersonating a Mexican impersonating an American. No, a Chicano is a perfected Mexican.

Plant #3: Gwermo, can you say something in Náhuatl?
GP: Ggggua . . . camole

Plant #1: To the young Chicano: Where did you get your tattoos? Chino? Folsom? They're real sexy.
RS: I got them in Knotts Berry Farm last week. Temporary, you know . . .

Plant #2: To the alien on the left: Do you have a green card?
GP: *(responds in tongues)*

Plant #3: Hey Roberto, can you please tell us what's the relationship between the Zapatistas, rap, L.A. gang culture, and the resurgence of Chicano nationalism?

RS: No.

Plant #1: Mr. Peña, I read in *Artforum* that you don't want to pay child support, and that you mistreat women artistic collaborators. Is that true?
GP: It must be true. Critics are always objective when they talk about my work.

(At this point audience members feel compelled to begin to ask other insensitive questions. For some reason, it never fails.)

RS: *(slowly gets pissed)* Come on, guys. What kind of questions are these? How about something more shocking? Let's tell some racist jokes. Would anyone like to share a racist joke? Come on, it's all part of the healing process. *(to GP)* Bill, you got any racist jokes? *(GP nods)* Come on everybody. Let's encourage this man to be brave. Órale vato, give us some racist stuff!

GP: Alright, alright! What do you call a Chicano baptism? . . . A bean dip! *(he laughs neurotically)*

RS: *(pissed)* That's not good enough. Come on, say something really offensive, motherfucker! Go on, say it!!

GP tries to speak, but is unable to. He laughs, cries, and falls on his knees. RS grabs a knife and stands behind him in a menacing manner. He brings the knife up as if getting ready to stab him.

RS: *(screaming)* What's the difference between a Mexican and a Cuban, eh?! *(no answer)* How many Mexican artists does it take to fill up a theater like this, eh?! You pathetic stereotype! You stand-up comedian wannabe . . .

BLACKOUT.

THREATENED, ENDANGERED, OR EXTINCT?

A) A threatened species is likely to become endangered within the foreseeable future.

B) An endangered species is in danger of extinction.

C) An extinct species no longer exists.

— *San Diego Natural History Museum*

Please, place the following species in the appropriate category:

Aztec	☐
Apache	☐
Seminole	☐
Taino	☐
Siboney	☐
Lacandon	☐
Chicano	☐
Garifuna	☐
Anglo-Saxon	☐
Marxist	☐

ON U.S./MEXICO RELATIONS:
From the Battle of El Alamo to the Signing of NAFTA

Dear ex-friend,
I'm saddened by the fact that we simply couldn't
    agree
in our first meeting
I wanted to talk about everything with a good cup
    of coffee
you wanted the meeting to be over quickly
I was too suave and talkative
you were plain rude & too direct for my chilango
    taste
I called you "gringo" de cariño
you called me "minority" twice
we didn't mean it, of course
but we were somehow damned by History
I politely overstated our differences
you tried to overlook all of them
I despised your lack of affection
you hated my touching you unnecessarily
I made you feel guilty
you made me feel inferior
I truly thought you needed some therapy
you thought I wanted a job real bad

we just couldn't reach a consensus
you kept looking at your watch
wondering why I was so flamboyant
— there is a certain strength in exhibitionism, ¿que
      no?
I wondered why you were so measured
— there is unquestionable power in being reserved
& when it came to cultural politics
we just couldn't see eye to eye
you pontificated that multiculturalism was
      rightfully dead
I replied that you were avoiding the crucial matters
      of race
you felt I was implying that you were a racist
& changed the subject & your tone of voice, just like
      that
you then placed too much importance on ecology
while I put too much emphasis on immigration
you were clearly unwilling to discuss colonial
      privilege
while I was unwilling (or perhaps unable) to discuss
      aesthetics
& worst of all, we simply couldn't laugh together
my jokes were too baroque & had no punchline
and yours were too brief & simplistic
we parted feeling utterly misunderstood

II
in our second encounter I arrived a half-hour late
you were pissed but didn't express it
you ordered raw vegetables & juice
I ordered pork, rum, and a humongous dessert

you were horrified
at the end of the dinner I pulled out my cigarettes
& you proceeded to lecture me on lung cancer &
      nonsmokers' rights
I was pissed but didn't express it
we simply couldn't find any common ground
during coffee — you had chamomile tea, by the
      way —
you finally expressed your resentment of my fame
you felt it had everything to do with the fact that I
      am Mexican
you said that in fact I was a "bad actor and a worse
      poet
who finds refuge in the fashionable kilombo of
      performance art"
I responded by bringing up the fact that you had
      tenure
in a system where only 3 percent of professors are
      people of color
you thought I had made up the statistics
I thought to myself: "this ex-sweet, liberal güerito
is in fact un backlasher de aquellas," but I swallowed
      my words
you then insisted I was a mere token for white
      liberals
I reminded you that more than half of my work
takes place in Chicano/Mexicano venues
you said, "that's not good enough"
I replied sarcastically, "sure, we're never good
      enough
you want me back in the margins
where no one can hear my voice, ¿que no?"

stuttering in anger you said I was "ungrateful to an
    art world
which has embraced me unconditionally"
I suggested you could read a mountain of reviews
by critics accusing me of the same things you were
but you said you needed no proof of anything
since there were probably twice as many reviews
complimenting me a-critically
at that point I pulled out my conceptual knife &
    stabbed you
I called you "a broken white male
with an acute case of compassion fatigue"
I didn't mean it, but I was pissed
you left the restaurant fuming
I had a Catholic guilt attack
and called you the next day to apologize
but you said our friendship was over
a week later, NAFTA was finally approved by
    Congress
& you went on vacation to Mazatlán
per omnia saecula saeculorum, amen.

15 WAYS OF RELATING ACROSS THE BORDER

between you & me . . .
no one else
tonight we are each other
miento
between you & me . . .
a page
and no scissors to cut it
miento
between you & me . . .
a twenty-mile-long poem
let's coedit it
miento
between you & me . . .
a knife pointing at me
and you don't even know my name
miento
between you & me . . .
a basic agreement
two plus two equals twenty
miento
between you & me . . .
billions of molecules
and nothing to be done about it

miento
between you & me . . .
a tunnel of hormones
come visit me tonight
miento
between you & me . . .
a downward spiral
let's dance
miento
between you & me . . .
another you & me
exchanging partners
miento
between you & me . . .
a political abyss
honey, don't even waste your time
miento
between you & me . . .
my iridescent penis
paraphrasing the umbilical cord
miento
between you & me . . .
a jungle of absurdities
let's meet some other day
miento
between you & me . . .
a massacre of animals
& you'd better give me an explanation
miento
between you & me . . .
a basic biological fact:
serpents & eagles don't mate

miento
between you & me . . .
a bottle of Meyers
let's drive through Hell right now

THE BORDER RUN

hen you're ready to cross over,
u run for the border.

Where you'll find tacos so
you can hear 'en

'goin' for food

danger zone/
terreno peligroso

Bust loose. Taco Bell has y
Anytime, any day

dinary fast food places,
d head for Taco Bell.

MAKE A RUN
FOR THE BORDER™

DANGER ZONE: Cultural Relations Between Chicanos and Mexicans at the End of the Century

I N FEBRUARY OF 1995, THE FIRST STAGE OF A BINATIONAL PERFOR-
mance project called "Terreno Peligroso/Danger Zone" was completed. For an entire month — two weeks in Los Angeles and two in
Mexico City — eleven experimental artists whose work challenges stereotypical and/or official notions of identity, nationality, language, sexuality,
and the creative process worked together daily. Representing Mexico were
Lorena Wolffer, Felipe Ehrenberg, Eugenia Vargas, César Martínez, and
Elvira Santamaría; from California were Elia Arce, Rubén Martínez, Nao
Bustamante, Luis Alfaro, Roberto Sifuentes, and myself. Chosen by the
curators and producers, Josefina Ramírez and Lorena Wolffer, this group
was as eclectic and diverse as our two cultures (Chicano and Mexican). The
performances were presented at the University of Calfornia at Los Angeles
(UCLA) and in the Ex-Teresa Arte Alternativo (Mexico City).

The performance work we did covered a wide spectrum, ranging
from the most intimate ritual actions to the most confrontational
activist performance; including tableaux vivants, avant-cabaret, spoken
word poetry, apocalyptic rituals, and street "interventions." Our goals
(at least those we consciously expressed) were: to create art together
(border art is collaborative by nature); to open the Pandora's box of
North/South relations and unleash the border demons; to destroy
taboos; and to replace simplistic views of cultural otherness with more
complex visions. The following text attempts to outline some of the
problems that the artists confronted during this binational encounter.

I

At the close of 1993, many artists of Latin American origin who were living in the United States ingenuously believed that NAFTA, or the *"Tratado de Libre Comer-se"* — despite its grave omissions in the areas of ecology, human and labor rights, culture, and education — would, at least indirectly, create the conditions for a rapprochement between Chicanos and Mexicans. But that idea completely backfired on us. Instead, ferocious nationalist movements began to arise in response to globalization of the economy and culture. Xenophobic proposals reminiscent of Nazi Germany — such as Operation Gatekeeper and California's chilling Proposition 187 — were brandished to confront the increasing and inevitable Mexicanization of the United States. We watched, perplexed, as the sudden opening of markets occurred almost simultaneously with the militarization of the border and the construction of a huge metal wall to separate several border cities. Capital, hollow dreams, and assembly plants easily crossed from one side to the other, but human beings — along with critical art and ideas — were prohibited passage. It seemed that culturally, as well as economically, the *maquiladora* model had been perfected: Mexicans would provide the raw material and do the arduous, badly paid work; Anglos would run the show; and Chicanos would be left out of the picture.

We are like tiny, insignificant spectators at a great end-of-the-century wrestling match: "The Invisible Octopus of Pseudo-internationalization vs. the Hydra of Neo-nationalism." Round One: The neoliberal formula of a continent unified by free trade, tourism, and digital high-technology is confronted by indigenous, campesino, environmental, and human rights movements. *Coitus interruptus.* The Mexican peso plummets, foreign capital flees, and the Marlboro dreams of neoliberal elites vanish in a cloud of sulfurous smoke. *Cambio.*

The crises are also becoming globalized. In the topography of the end-of-the-century crisis, Bosnia is strangely connected to Los

Angeles (L.A.- Herzegovina), just as Chiapas is connected to the Basque country and to Northern Ireland. Mexicans in California confront a dilemma similar to that faced by Palestinians and black South Africans, and the young people of Mexico City (members of Generation MEX) manifest the same existential and psychological illnesses that plague New Yorkers or Berliners.

The paradoxes multiply *loca*rhythmically. In the era of computers, faxes, virtual reality, World Beat, and "total television" (à la CNN), it has become increasingly difficult for us to communicate across the borders of culture and language. The smaller and more concentrated the world becomes, the more foreign and incomprehensible it seems to us. We are now exposed to many languages, but we lack the keys to translation. We have access to incredible amounts of information, but we don't have the codes to decipher it. The seductive virtual universe, with its unlimited options and multidirectional promises, confounds our ability to order information and to act in the world with ethical and political clarity.

If anything could be said to define "postmodernity," it is the steady increase in symptoms of border culture, the endless syncretisms with a complete lack of synchronicity, misencounters, and misunderstandings: "I am, as long as you (as the representative of racial, linguistic, or cultural otherness) no longer are"; "I cross, therefore you exist (or vice versa)"; "Fuck you, therefore I am"; and others that would be better left unsaid. Contemporary art — at its most critical, irreverent, and experimental — is an involuntary chronicle of the ontological and epistemological confusion that is affecting all of us equally.

Chicano rap, Mexican alternative rock, independent cinema, and performance art converge on these key points: the brave acceptance of our transborderized and denationalized condition; the *ars poetic* of vertigo; the metaphysics of fragmentation; and the total collapse of linear logic, dramatic time, and narrative aesthetics. (This book is hopefully an example of this.)

II

The myths that once grounded our identity have become bankrupt. Sixties-era pan-Latinamericanism, *la mexicanidad* (unique, monumental, undying), and Chicanismo (with thorns and a capital C) have all been eclipsed by processes of cultural borderization and social fragmentation. Like it or not, we are now denationalized, de-mexicanized, transchicanized, and pseudo-internationalized. And worse, in fear of falling into a new century we refuse to assume this new identity, roaming around instead in a Bermuda Triangle. We live in economic uncertainty, terrorized by the holocaust of AIDS, divided (better yet, trapped) by multiple borders, disconnected from ourselves and others by strange mass cultures and new technologies that appeal to our most mediocre desires for instant transformation and psychological expansion.

In this bizarre landscape, politics becomes pop culture, and technology turns into folklore. Mass culture, popular culture, and folklore are no longer distinguishable from one another: it seems that our only true community is television. Perhaps our only real nation is also television. Mexico is, and continues to be "one" by virtue of television; without television perhaps it would cease to be. Televisa is Mexico's macro-Ministry of Communications, Culture, and Binational Tourism, all in one. In the United States of the '90s, the most famous Mexicans are TV personalities such as Gloria Trevi, Paco Stanley, "Verónica," and Raúl Velasco. Sadly, the main connection that Mexican immigrants maintain with that marvelous, imaginary country called Mexico is via soap operas. If we are familiar with "El Sup" (Subcomandante Marcos) and Superbarrio, it's because they are skillful manipulators of the symbolic (and performative) politics of the media. In this context, we "untelevisable" performance artists are asking ourselves what role will be left for us to perform in the immediate future. Maybe our only options will be to make conceptual commercials for MTV and/or appear in artsy rock videos. For the moment, I'm having a hard time imagining more dignified alternatives.

III

North Americans (in the United States) used to define their identity in direct opposition to the "Soviet threat." With the end of the Cold War, the United States fell into an unprecedented identity crisis. Today its place in the world is uncertain and its (fictitious) enemies are multiplying left and right. On the eclectic list of recent anti-American "others" one finds fundamentalist Muslims, Japanese businessmen, Latin American drug lords, black rap musicians, and more recently, "illegal aliens" in both senses of the word: cultural martians invading "our" institutions, and seditious laborers who are "stealing jobs from *real* Americans."

This identity crisis translates into an immense nostalgia for an (imaginary) era in which people of color didn't exist, or at least when we were invisible and silent. The political expression of this nostalgia is chilling: "Let's take our country back." The far right, like Pete Wilson, Newt Gingrich, Jesse Helms, and Pat Buchanan, along with many Democrats, are in agreement on the following: This country must be saved from chaos and collapse into Third-Worldization; "illegal" immigrants must be deported; the poor should be put in jail (three strikes, you're out); welfare, affirmative action, and bilingual education programs must be dismantled; and the cultural funding infrastructure that has been infiltrated by "liberals with leftist tendencies" (the National Endowment for the Arts and the Humanities and the Corporation for Public Broadcasting) must be decimated. In the euphemistic Contract with America, ethnic "minorities," independent artists and intellectuals, the homeless, the elderly, children, and especially immigrants from the South, are all under close watch.

In Mexico, ever since the implementation of NAFTA the border no longer functions as the great barrier of contention against which official Mexican identity is defined. This has created its own large-scale identity crisis. Without the continuous harassment from Washington's

Power Rangers, the *yupitecas* and the *mariachis* have had no other alternative than to go off to a cantina and drown themselves in the depths of lost love and *neo-Porfirista* nostalgia. The social explosion in Chiapas has complicated things further and has literally torn the country in two. *Salinista* Mexico preferred to think of itself as *posmoderno* and international, desiring at all costs to look outward and northward, but the unfolding internal political crisis has forced the country's gaze back inward to confront its racism against indigenous peoples and its abysmal contradictions.

Although the roots of our crises are of a very different nature, both Califas (California) and Tenochtitlán (Mexico City) are living through unprecedented identity crises. And, for the first time in the twentieth century there is a growing consciousnesss on both sides of the border that the crises and dangers that we're undergoing are similar. This mutual recognition could be the basis for new, more profound cultural relations between Chicanos and Mexicans: If we recognize that we're all equally screwed, perhaps at the same time we are equally capable of greater compassion and mutual understanding.

IV

At present, the only thing that unites those who left Mexico and those who stayed is our inability to understand and accept our inevitable differences. We detect the existence of these invisible borders, but we are unable to articulate them, much less cross them with tact. This phenomenon is clearly evident in the area of cultural relations between Mexico and the United States, most especially, between Mexicans and Chicanos. It's here where the contradictions abound, where the wound opens and bleeds, and the poisoned subtext of mutual (and largely fictional) resentments rises to the surface.

We, the post-Mexican and Chicano artists from "over there/the other side" look to the South with a certain ingenuousness, a distorting nostalgia and admiration, always dreaming of our possible return. Meanwhile, the Mexicans who remain south of the border look at us with a combination of desire and repudiation, fear and condescension. The mirrors are always breaking. While we on the California coast — where the West literally ends — look toward the Pacific, those in Mexico City look attentively toward Europe and New York. (The paradox here is that Europe and New York — in spiritual and artistic bankruptcy — are carefully watching both Chicanos and Mexicans, searching for novelty, inspiration, and exoticism to decorate the blank walls of their nihilist crisis.)

The missed encounters continue. In the United States, Latino artists work in the flammable context of the multicultural wars and identity politics. We define ourselves as a culture of resistance, and in our eagerness to "resist the dominant culture" we frequently lose all sense of a continental perspective, and end up assuming ethnocentric and separatist positions. Meanwhile, the Mexican artistic communities — with some exceptions — are undergoing a stage of nonreflective extroversion and the rejection of textually political or politicized art, which they associate with "minor" art and with official Mexican cultural discourse. Although they are the protagonists and witnesses of their country's most serious crisis in modern history (perhaps comparable to that of Eastern Europe), many Mexican experimental artists have chosen not to "textually" use *la crisis* as subject matter in their work. Right now, they are more inclined to create a personal, intimate art of an existential or neoconceptual style.

When Mexican artists "go North," they do so with the intention of breaking into the commercial gallery circuit. They are prejudiced by the the solemnity and virtual failure of official cultural exchange projects, and to them Chicano art appears didactic, reiterative, and poorly executed. Our themes — racism, immigration, the obsessive deconstruction of identities, and the subversion of media stereotypes of Mexicans — seem distant and irrelevant to their purely "Mexican" reality.

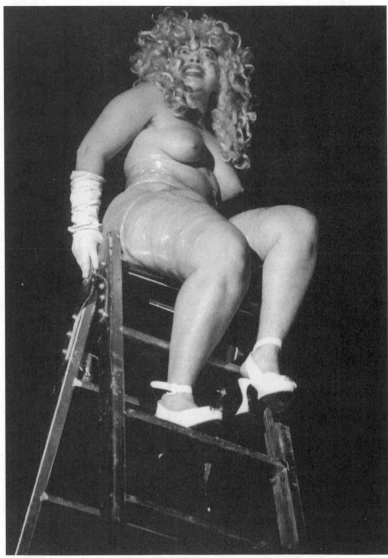

Nao Bustamante performing "America the Beautiful" at Ex-Teresa
Arte Alternativo, Mexico City, 1995. Photo by Monica Naranjo

They seem not to fully grasp the magnitude of their own crisis, and refuse (not entirely without reason) to be seen as a "minority." The Chicanos, hypersensitive to this fragile relationship, feel rejected by the Mexicans, and the gap between the two cultures grows wider.

The long and convoluted history of cultural exchange between Chicanos and Mexicans can be translated as a chronicle of missed encounters. For fifteen years Chicanos have tried, without success, to "return" through the great door and to reconcile themselves with their Mexican relatives. With few exceptions, the reception to their art has been openly hostile or, at best, paternalistic. Despite the numerous and fashionable projects of binational interchange facilitated (or inspired) by NAFTA, Mexico's predominant vision of Chicano art is still antiquated. In 1995, most Mexicans still believe that all Chicano artists make barrio murals, write protest poetry, and erect neon altars to Frida Kahlo and the Virgin of Guadalupe; that they all speak like Edward Olmos in *American Me* and dance to Tex-Mex music; that they all drive low-riders. They ignore the actual diversity and complexity of our communities, and remain unaware of the influence of the Central American, Caribbean, and Asian communities that have moved into the Chicano neighborhoods. The influence of gay and lesbian communities of color, with their challenge to the excessive dose of testosterone from which Chicano culture has suffered for the last two decades, is also completely overlooked. The processes that have brought us to more fluid and interactive models of a Chicano/Latino multi-identity are still unheard of in Mexico City, and two generations of young artists who have publicly questioned conventional, static notions of Chicanismo remain outside of the realm of most Mexicans' consciousness.

V

In 1995, *la mexicanidad* and the Latino/Chicano experience are becoming completely superimposed. The 200,000 Mexicans who cross the border every month bring us fresh and constant reminders of our past (for Mexican Americans, the continual migratory flow functions as a sort of collective memory). And the opposite phenomenon also happens: the mythic North (which represents the future) also returns to the South, searching for its lost past. Many of the Mexicans who come to "the other side" become "chicanized" and return to Mexico — either on their own or by force of the immigration authorities. In the act of returning they contribute to the silent process of Chicanization which Mexico is currently undergoing.

This dual dynamic, as expressed in popular culture, functions as a sort of X-ray of the social psyche: the "northern" sounds of *quebradita* (a fusion of north Mexican *banda* and techno-pop) and rap can already be heard from Yucatán to Chihuahua; while the songs of Mexican bands such as Los Caifanes, La Lupita, Maldita Vecindad, and Los Tigres del Norte are being hummed from San Diego to New York. Selena, the "queen of Tex-Mex" (RIP), is venerated in both countries. The sounds of "tecno-banda" and *quebradita* (no one can deny that these are immigrant sounds) re-mexicanize Chicano music. The "cholos" and the "salvatruchos" (young Salvadorans in L.A.) are wearing Stetson hats and cowboy boots, while Aztec punk-rockers in Mexico City, Guadalajara, and Tijuana are expropriating Chicano iconography and fashion, and talking in Spanglish, ¿que no?

Mexican identity (or better said, the many Mexican identities) can no longer be explained without the experience of "the other side," and vice versa. As a socio-cultural phenomenon, Los Angeles simply cannot be understood without taking Mexico City — its southernmost neighborhood — into account. Between both cities runs the greatest migratory axis on the planet, and the conceptual freeway with the greatest number of accidents.

As transnationalized artists, our challenge is to recompose the fragmented chronicle of this strange end-of-the-century phenomenon. And so, the performance begins . . .

translated by Clifton Ross

DES-ENCUENTRO DE 3 MUN-2

. . . para Angel Cosmos, compita en el más allá

(This conceptual poem in Spanglish was proposed as the text for an anti-Columbus "intercontinental tourist poster" at the Universidad de la Rábida in Spain.)

> México en Aztlán
> Califas en Spa-ña
> Ex-paña en Mé-xico
> Triángulo de las Ver-mudas/triangle
> Palos buenos pa'los malos
> Calógicamente hablando digo
> El Viejo Mundo
> se imagina pus-moderno
> El Nuevo, se reinventa
> en la contigüidad
> contínuo, sin-tínuo sin ti no
> te
> tenepantla tinemi tajoditzin
> untranslatable sablazo
> against the New World Order
> trans-afloat
> the Great Atlantic border

border fronteraabordo y desembarco.
asss I wasssaying last night
de Palo en Palo hasta el Caribe
taíno non plus ultra fornicare
de Veracrúz a Tenochtitlán
de Mexicou Cida a Tijuana-Nirvana
de Lost Angeles a San Antonio
and güey beyond
de Manhattan a Madrid
& then to Sevilla & back again
to Palos
two palitos can make one child
o one poema en su defecto
so I defect. caput.
mañana retorno a Califas.

Right: Still from *Neutron*, a Mexican B-movie.

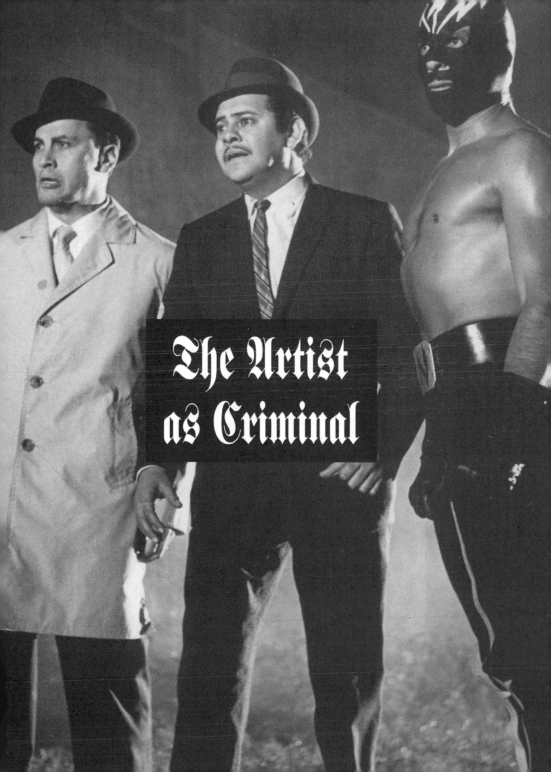

The Artist
as Criminal

THE ARTIST AS CRIMINAL

I VIVIDLY REMEMBER THAT COLD AFTERNOON IN BUENOS AIRES. MY colleague Coco Fusco and I were performing a version of our project, "The Guatinaui World Tour" right on the corner of Callao and Corrientes, one of the most frequented corners in the city. As part of our performance projects subverting the colonial formats of the "living diorama" and pseudo-ethnographic exhibitions of humans, we spent three days inside a gilded cage displaying ourselves as "exotic primitives" from a fictitious island in the Gulf of Mexico. Suddenly, from within the crowd, a mysterious character appeared, sprinkled me with liquid, and then disappeared. Seconds later, I realized I had been the victim of a physical assault. My stomach had been burned with acid.

One of the many theories circulating in the Buenos Aires artistic community speculated that this attack involved a misunderstanding. The assailant must have thought that our project was a direct commentary on Argentine military culture (which jailed thousands of youths before the alleged democratic transition of 1987) and felt himself implicated.

For politicized border artists experimenting with the tenuous and ever-fluctuating frontiers between art and life, there is always a real danger present; especially when the artwork occurs outside of the protected space of cultural institutions. In other words, it's one thing to carry out iconoclastic actions in a theater or museum for a public that is predisposed to tolerate radical behavior, and it's quite another to bring the same work into the street and introduce it into the mined terrain of unpredictable social and political forces. In the street, the risks are far greater. Some of these are obvious, such as confronting the intolerance of the police, the army, or extremist groups. Others are more random, like a surprise encounter with a lunatic who happens to cross your path. Performance artists are well aware of these risks, but every now and then we don't accurately gauge the climate of the context or the symbolic weight of our actions.

In mid-July of 1994, I received a disturbing telephone call. The artist Hugo Sánchez (who shares his name with a Mexican soccer star), a native of Ciudad Obregón, Sonora, longtime resident of Tijuana, and current resident of Culiacán, Sinaloa, had just been deported to — not from — the city of San Diego for "desecrating the Mexican flag" in a performance. The newspapers, including the infamous Mexican tabloid *El Alarma,* published scandalous images and headlines portraying the norteño artist as a psychopath.

The facts, hallucinatory as they are, are the following:

On July 11, Hugo Sánchez arrived in Tijuana to participate in the filming of *Fronterilandia,* codirected by Rubén Ortiz (from Mexico) and Jesse Lerner (from the United States), and sponsored by the Fundación Cultural Mexicana [Mexican Cultural Foundation]. The film-makers describe the work as "an experimental chronicle, half documentary and half poetic essay, of the mythical perceptions which both sides of the border have about each other."

The directors planned to shoot a performance by Hugo Sánchez, using the streets of Tijuana as a backdrop. The portion of the work to be filmed focused on the topic of migration. The hybrid character played by Sánchez was a type of "undocumented Zapatista/*charro* [cowboy]," decked out in a mariachi sombrero à la "TJ curio-style," a ski mask, a flag wrapped around his chest, with a cow's head, representing, in the artist's words, "the pain of the emigrants who cross the border daily and who are sacrificed like animals by an inhuman work/police system."

Filming began early on July 12. The crew consisted of only a cameraman, a photographer, and a sound technician. The two opening scenes were filmed without mishap; the first in front of an extremely strange edifice in the shape of an Ionic column which is known as the "Wadah," and the second next to the Monument to the Freedom of Expression. After these sequences were filmed, the group made its way over to the Monument to the Textbook (located in front of the Lázaro Cárdenas School). The crew prepared to shoot a scene in which Hugo was to insert nails into the cow's tongue (which came out of his mouth, appearing to be his own tongue) as a commentary on "the pain engendered by the misunderstandings between races and countries." Lights, camera, action. Suddenly, Ricardo Luna and Jorge Nava, two agents from the municipal police, appeared. The filmmakers showed them a letter from the Fundación sponsoring the project, explaining that it was "a cultural project, not a political action." The policemen had lost their patience and their sense of humor, and decided to arrest Hugo Sánchez under suspicion of "disrespect for the flag." Many patrols arrived and all hell broke loose.

Since Hugo was being charged with a federal offense, he was immediately transferred to the office of the Federal Prosecutor (PGR). Tabloid photographers surrounded the "Zapatista cowboy" and captured his rage and confusion — flash, click, *Alarma* style. Eagerly they took close-ups of the cow's head and of the sacrosanct "bloodstained" flag. Subsequently, the police transferred the performance artist to a clinic for drug addicts and people with psychological disorders. Fortunately, after a meticulous examination, the doctor declared that the artist was "neither a drug addict, nor crazy." Upon being returned to the cells of the PGR, Hugo was subjected to a full body search amid the constant insults of the law-enforcement officers. As a protest, he decided to go on a hunger strike.

The deputies found a U.S. passport in the artist's clothes. Hugo explained that "although I was born and have always lived on Mexican territory, my mother made me a nationalized North American when I was young . . . just like millions of other border Mexicans." The officials confiscated Hugo's passport, and decided he was "Chicano, not a Mexican."

On July 13, through the desperate efforts of Hugo's friends, various organizations got wind of the situation. Representatives of the National Committee of Human Rights, the Casa de la Cultura de Tijuana, and the Tijuana Cultural Center began to pressure the PGR for Hugo's release. Also on that day, the artist had to present his version of events before the legislator Socorro López. Hugo contended that he "never had the intention of desecrating the flag" and that, paradoxically, the performance had been conceived as "a patriotic gesture of symbolic defense of the Mexican emigrants who daily risk their lives crossing the dangerous border." Ms. López burst out laughing.

The PGR authorities got in touch with agents from Mexican immigration, and together they decided that the artist (who has devoted much of his life to defending undocumented workers) was "illegally" dwelling in Mexico (his native land). Hugo's risks were multiplying. As he was considered a "foreigner," the insult to the flag would have more serious consequences for him. He was alerted to the real possibility of becoming "persona non grata" under Article 33 of the Mexican Constitution, which would forbid him from ever setting foot in Mexican territory again. He was transferred to the sinister prison known as "la ocho," where they locked him up with other "foreigners." His deportation proceedings began.

On the morning of July 14, a (Hispanic) representative from the U.S. Consulate visited Hugo Sánchez in his cell. Hugo was told not to worry, that soon he would "return to his country." Hugo tried to explain that "his country" was Mexico, and it was there that he wished to remain. The consular envoy didn't get it.

On July 15, accompanied by an agent from Mexican immigration and a deputy, Hugo was transferred to the Customs Office of the City of Tijuana. There, he was required to pay a fine "for being a foreigner and acting in a Mexican film without being in possession of the appropriate permits." Fortunately, a curator from the Tijuana Cultural Center telephoned the agents and convinced them not to fine the artist, arguing that "people don't make money doing this type of art (performance)."

Hours later, Hugo was finally handed over to the U.S. Immigration and Naturalization Service authorities. *"Maestro,"* Hugo told me, "for the first time in my life, the *migra* gave me a hero's welcome. They even gave me lunch money. It's like I just walked into a mirror where reality's turned upside-down."

Later, on the same day of his deportation, the exhausted and humiliated artist decided to return to Tijuana "illegally" and confront the Mexican authorities. He went to District Court No. 7 to inquire about his case and the whereabouts of his passport. The judge was "on vacation." An employee who had read about the "case of the lunatic in the newspaper," assured him that he would receive a summons to appear in court, and warned him that he "should be prepared to receive, according to the judge's discretion, either four years in prison (in Mexico) or permanent deportation."

As befits the hair-raising paradox of this binational thriller, Hugo's first court date was set for September 18, two days after the celebration of the Mexican Declaration *(Grito)* of Independence. When September came, he was notified of a change of date; this time he was set to appear in court on October 11, one day before the alleged "discovery of America," which is known in Mexico as *Día de la Raza* (birth of the mestizo race). A few days later, Hugo's court date was postponed indefinitely. Desperate and penniless, Hugo decided to cross the border and await the new date in his (fictitious) country of origin. Mexico, his true country, had been transformed into a juridical nightmare out of a Chicano Secret Service *pochonovela.*

Hugo Sánchez's case is unique: a Mexican deported to the United States for doing a performance. Why? Perhaps it had to do with the politically charged context. It was an extremely tense time in Tijuana:

the assassinations of the ruling party's presidential candidate Colosio and of Tijuana's chief of police Benítez had created a pervasive climate of melancholy, mistrust, and fear that affected everyone. Perhaps it was the timing of the incident, one month before the Mexican elections scheduled for August 21, which the opposition party had a real possibility of winning (Tijuana was in the hands of the opposition at that time). But other, inescapable, extracontextual factors are also part of the picture. The police's intolerance for alternative culture, and the heavy restrictions on freedom of expression in Mexico definitely contributed to Sánchez's Kafkaesque nightmare. Sadly, in an authoritarian society that so desperately wants to consider itself the eternal protagonist of a transition to democracy, the borders between art and illegality are becoming increasingly thin.

In a letter of support for the Mexican artist, the Chicano artist and writer Rubén Guevara wrote: "Hugo Sánchez's performance was as 'offensive' as the social conditions that inspired it. The artist is nothing if not a catalyst of social and cultural forces, and his work is a simple, stylized reflection of reality. . . . The shameful judgment passed on Sánchez is a test of the new government's (Zedillo's) democratic image. . . . The test consists precisely in allowing *any* cultural gesture, however radical or strange it may seem to be, not just tolerated, but respected."

Thanks to media pressure (including publication of this essay in Mexico's national daily newspaper *La Jornada*), the judge decided to dismiss Hugo's case in December. The passport disappeared mysteriously from the Mexicali archives. (Maybe now there is a third "Hugo Sánchez" wandering the streets of San Diego, Los Angeles, or San Francisco.)

The challenge for Hugo Sánchez now (the performance artist, that is) is to overcome his fear of using the street as a laboratory for artistic creation, and to recover his fragile and bruised Mexican identity. As for me, only a scar on my right leg remains as a sinister memory of the dangers involved in doing performance in the '90s.

translated by Christopher Winks

La Hora Nostálgica de las Dedicatorias

Para: Linda Rondstadt, Honcha Latinette
Rola: "El Bolero de la Coors"
From: Torcidos e Incrédulos de Chino

Para: Helmut Kohl
Rola: "Sin Fronteras"
From: Los Tigres del Norte
(Nota: Despues de 1848 nos dejaron hipotecados los muy cabrones.
Any suggestions Mr. Kohl? You know about borders, que no?)

Para Salman Rushdie y Andrés Serrano
Rola: "La Bala Perdida"
From: El Ayatollah Helms y el trio Los Tapados

Para: Major Riordan de Lost Angeles
Rola: "The Big One"
From: La trova de Saint Andreas

Para: Charlie Salinas, el "no mames hunger striker"
Rola: "When Did It All Go Wrong"
From: El Comanche Marcos y la Banda Tormenta del Suroeste

Para: O.J.
Rola: "When You Thought You Had It Made"
(de Willy Nelson y Julio Iglesias)
From: The Crips & the Bloods (L.A. County Jail, Crujía #20)

Para: Selena, la Reina del Norte
Rola: "Hasta Que la Muerte Nos Reuna"
From: All the bleeding hearts in the southlands

Para: La Sad Eyes de Tepoztlán
Rola: "Ya Crúzate Cabrona" (corrido)
From: El Charromántico, inconsolable en Aztlán

To request a dedicatoria, dial 1-800-naftart

Why are "you" so scared of "us"?

Illustration by "Sergio," courtesy of *Teen Angel* Magazine

TRADITIONAL BOLEROS . . .

BÉSAME MUCHO

kiss me, kiss moi my chola
como si fuera esta noche the last migra raid
kiss me, kiss moi mi chuca
que tengo miedo perderte somewhere in L.A.

watcha' que maybe mañana yo estare en la pinta
longing for your ass (digo eyes)
y que quizá me deporten de nuevo a Tijuana
por ser ilegal

EL REY DEL CRUCE

una yerba en el camino
me enseño que mi destino
era cruzar y cruzar

por ahí me dijo un troquero
que no hay que cruzar primero
pero hay que saber cruzar

con tarjeta o sin tarjeta
digo yo la pura neta
y mi palabra es la ley . . .

no tengo troca ni jaina
ni raza que me respalda
pero sigo siendo de L.A.

Gómez-Peña as "El Mariachi–Liberace" at the Brooklyn Academy of Music, 1991.
Photo by Jeffrey Henson Scales

the last migration

THE LAST MIGRATION: A Spanglish Opera (in progress)

T HE STAGING OF THIS TEXT REQUIRES A CAST OF APPROXIMATELY fifteen performers (including performance artists, actors, dancers, opera singers, classical and norteño musicians, and rockeros). Basic technical support includes two large video screens with projectors, an SPX sound mixer, five ghetto blasters, levelier microphones, and the necessary sound equipment for the musicians.

Some preliminary staging ideas: In the center of the stage, with religious lighting on him, is a crucified gang member on a wooden cross; above him, a huge video screen showing Mexican and Japanese B-movies, as well as assorted preproduced performance vignettes. Dozens of dead chickens hang from the ceiling at different heights. A live "end-of-the-century chamber orchestra" includes two opera singers, a rapper, a Tex-Mex accordion player, a rock guitarist, a cellist, and five ghetto blasters. Two digital-read-out display bars translate/mistranslate excerpts of the texts into English, Spanish, and/or French.

Parts of the text will be delivered live by Gómez-Peña and the other performers. Other parts will be sung by the opera singers or by the rapper. Certain texts will be prerecorded as audio or video. Not all of the following texts will be utilized for the stage version, and certainly not in the order they appear here. Movement and actions will be developed during rehearsals with the cast. A two-month residency would be ideal for staging this piece.

INTRO: INDIAN PROPHECY

PRERECORDED VOICE/JUXTAPOSED WITH TONGUES:
Kalli, Mikiztli, Califas . . .
there will soon be a time
when the hearts, minds, & genitals of the White Bears
will be entirely covered with bruises
and for them, going through the motions of life
will be the worst punishment a living creature has
   ever endured
their pain, displayed as a daily spectacle on TV
and their only consolation,
to drink themselves to sleep
or to enroll in a motivational workshop
these are the nasty words of the Great Nahual . . .

and soon there will also be a time
when you & I aren't around anymore
and others will have to keep the window open

I: TRAINING TO FACE THE END OF THE CENTURY

SOUND OF CROWS, MIXED WITH MEXICAN ROCK 'N' ROLL.

It's Sunday on my L.A. balcony
it smells like gasoline and smoke
in geo-poetical terms,
I follow my instincts, my boots,
my tongue, my wicked desire
propelled by the winds of migration & memory
I exchange knives with my 12 performance selves
& then I jump rope to the beat of La Cuca
I'm training,
to face the end of the century

the stage is empty tonight
America in ruins
Anglo-America decrépita
radio static fills the air

RADIO STATIC.

II: PERFORMANCE

GREGORIAN CHANTS MIXED WITH RAP MUSIC.

I sit naked on a wheelchair
wearing a NAFTA wrestling mask
my chest is covered with pintas
shit like:

> *"los chucos también aman"*
> *"me dicen el jalapeño pusher"*
> *"Aztlán es pure genitalia"*
> *"the bells are ringing in Baghdad"*
> *"greetings from Ocosingo"*
> *"don't worry; be Hopi"*
> *"burritos unidos hasta la muerte"*
> *"no one can like a Mexican"*
> *"la ganga no morirá"*
> *"New Orleans ain't my barrio"*
> *"Selena, forever reina"*
> *"to die is to perform the last strip-tease"*

enigmatic pintas, may I say
say, say, say . . .
(I try to speak but I can't)
I can barely speak tonite:
(I whisper into the mike)
dear audience
ease my pain
lick my chest, my sweat, my blood
500 years of bleeding . . .
from head to toes
& all the way down to the root
I bleed
from Alaska to Patagonia
y me pesa un chingo decirlo
pero sangro
de inflación, dolor y dólar
de inflamación existencial
y mexicanidad insatisfecha
sangro
de tanto vivir en los United
de tanto luchar contra la migra
de tanto y tanto crossing borders
sangro, luego existo
parto, luego soy
soy
soy porque somos
we are un fuckin' chingo
the transient generation acá
from Los Angeles to the Bronx & far beyond
we, the mega "WE,"
we cry

"Border Brujo" prays to La Virgen del Cruce. Sushi, San Diego, 1989.
Photo by Becky Cohen

MEXICAN WALTZ MUSIC.

Five naked Zapatistas mop the floor in slow motion.

therefore the moon . . .
demanding restoration
tonight . . .
the moon . . .
is . . .
cracking . . .
up . . .
and you,
whoever you may be
are looking for an angry lover

III: LA PRAYER DEL FREEWAY 5
untranslatable, ni pedo

2 A.M. solitario at 90 miles an hour
I drive en trance, therefore I pray:
PREACHERLIKE VOICE:
Santa María, mother of dos
ruega por nos/otros los cruzadores
Tía Juana patrona de cruces y entrepiernes
ruega por ambas orillas y orificios
San Dollariego, patrón de migras y verdugos
ruega por tí mismo culero
Señora Porcupina de Los Angeles
líbranos del fuego y los deslaves
        y deporta a estos gueros plix
Santa Barbara, vírgen de nalgas tatuadas
psss prexta babe, tu chante pseudo-colonial
San Francisco de Asísmo, patrón de motos y terremotos

invita al mitote man
Santa Rosa, Madre del Crímen Letal,
líbranos de las balas anónimas
period.
santos y santas de fín de siglo
que habitan el olimpo del Art-maggeddon
comáos vivos entre vous
pero abran paso que ahí les voy
per omnia saecula saeculerosssss
sssstop!
(el fin del mundo
se encuentra
al final de la autopista)

IV: RADIO BROADCAST

OTHER VOICES, IN CHORUS, BEGIN:
> *"boat people/snake people/wandering incógnitos*
> *tar people/corn people/wandering raquíticos"*

Me . . .
Mex,
Mexique
Mexi-cannibal colega
I ask you tête-à-tête,
why are you so scared of the flames & the bad weather?
do immigrants remind you of unspoken wounds?
are you expecting my wolves to go away with the century?
was I supposed to disappear in Chinatown?
were you looking through the window when the
         boat people arrived?
were you?
'cause I was
their hearts were mine for an instant

in their eyes,
I saw my uncles
Pepe, Carlos, & Lolita
when they began to depart
half a century ago
from D.F. to Los Angeles
& then to Michigan and Canada
aaayyyyy!!
I was still imaginary sperma
but I remember somehow
(I subvocalize; then I mumble as if I was mentally handicapped)
my past, passado, passadísimo
part one of this Califassssaga:
"performance as random memory"

V: LOVE LETTER IN SPANGLISH . . .

dear X enmascarada
reina de los caminos bloqueados
this is a love song for you
la última
the song of the triple end
(the decade/the century/the milennium)
& it starts like this:

RAP MUSIC.

full moon, tape rolling . . . rrrrrolando
ain't living no more sin pecado
        "sin = pecado"
        "mea culpa de tanto mear"
— he wrote on an alley wall
so crunch my bones chuca sin patria

squeeze my ñonga Stolisnaya
fagocítame, traqueo-invádeme
draculébrame, amortájame con tape
que life is a dangerous vacation
a one-way ticket to East Timor,
San Salvador ou Port au Prince,
L.A./Herzegovina
or any other global set for our despair
decía . . .
dear X enmascarada,
wherever you may be
don't ever let me part again
porque si parto, ahora si,
yo-me-la y te-la ppppparto
ay!! my broken heart
literally, clinically broken
el mapa mundi,
cracked open on a surgical table

A BITTER VOICE SINGS IN THE BACKGROUND:
". . . y volver, volver, volver
a Califas otra vez . . ."

VI: LOVE LETTER CONTINÚA

(continúo con voz mas tierna y contenida)
I devoted years to your pubis Raramuri
a lifetime in the sphincter of America
scratched your back to the rolas of El Flaco
wrote you poems on airline vomit bags
stuff like . . .

"llorar políglota
to cry en inglés
entre íngles extranjeras
recordar en español
orar en lenguas muertas
rocanrolear en esperanto
signos todos de Nova Identidad
(ay, quanta concentrazione e necessaria
per parlare, e per togliere
la parole da dentro)"
wait, said my tongue en inglés
I meant to write in español
but I suddenly fffffforgot
sign:
el post—colonial warrior
servidor que cruza y nunca llega
P.S. #1:
Califas is burning again
Califas is burning
fade out
P.S. #2:
bruja, se me olvidaba
tu ya no rifas en mi lengua
since you scratched my heart
I just can't love you any more
(Balinese rock blasts out of my heart)
P.S. #3:
cansado estoy
y cansado permanezco
por los siglos de los siglos
let me loose

VII: UNTRANSLATABLE NOCHE DE ROL

MUSIC BY AUSTRALIAN BAND, *THE UMBRELLAS.*

cameras #1 & 2 rolling . . .
NASAL VOICE:
"the Aztec mummy strikes back"
Chapter One of the end of the begining
of the end of America, ca, ca, ca . . . put
NORMAL VOICE:
punto. inútil buscar la claridad
es el año del noventa y tres
y los buitres andan sueltos.

"MEXICO LINDO" BLUES.

SOFT VOICE:
. . . por lo tanto
en esta negra noche de amor minusválido
forrado en mi borrega me la rifo
busco la muerte de la identidad
la última frontera de occidente
las oldies del 105.7 AM
busco a ciegas/me tropiezo
descubro pintas y placazos
choros y aquelarres en la octava
estreno neologismos para abrirme brecha
pene-trading la oscuridad
sigo buscando . . .
el texto que tanta falta nos hace
la evidencia irrefutable de la caída del imperio
escucho voces de viejas masacres:
Plymouth, Tlaltelolco, Wounded Knee
(El Alamo no pinta en esta historia)

palabras en lenguas muertas:
ARCO, Sanyo, Mobil Oil
(I speak in tongues)
trans-míto en vivo desde nowhere
mensajes digitales pa' los vatos
los que habitan el instersticio
y la gran pausa
busco y encuentro:
brusco desencuentro
incapaz de traducir . . .

mistranslation:
something is missing here
something is out of control
somewhere in Mexico-Tenochtitlán
my mother is listening to Zappa
cut!!

(I try to say the following text but I make mistakes over & over)
I, I, I, can't pretend
this is translatable my dear
I just . . . can't . . . pretend . . . 'cause . . . tonight
my tongue is bleeding . . . tonight
but my tongue, amphibian tongue
lingua poluta, disoluta, is also yours
truly yours.
      firma: El Existentialist Mojado

VIII: NINTENDO

VIDEO SCREEN PLAYS A GODZILLA MOVIE.
SOUNDTRACK: QUEBRADITA MUSIC MIXED WITH HELICOPTERS.

COMPUTERIZED VOICE:
the Aztec mummy walks across America
mosquito migra choppers circle her head
techno-banda music erupts like magma
("la noche que Chicago se murió")
Godzilla appears on the horizon
la miiggrraaaaaaaaaaa!!
delete . . .
187 culebras
contra la voluntad de la historia
delete . . .
un mexicano menos
delete . . .
(computer crash)

IX: ANONYMOUS MESSAGE ON THE
ANSWERING MACHINE

FILTERED VOICE:
América masculla SOS . . .
no esss
U.S.
you sir!
GRINGOÑOL:
yyyouu serrr . . .
que ío soy poeta de mojados
illegal at heart
undocumented by birth
sospechoso por tradición

NORMAL VOICE:
thus I suggest that you die in Brazil
on the last night of Carnival
or perhaps in an orgy at Lake Atitlán
desprevenido, finiseculeando
so Mister Generic Gabacho,
turn off your television and essssscape
if not
the natural & social forces en contuvernio
will eventually get you
desprevenido, finiseculeando
digo, it's your karma man
(end of message)

X: AFTER THE POW-WOW

when the pow-wow was over,
— broken bottles of Bohemia on the ground
a young mechista dared to ask Gran Vato Crying Wolf:
"what do you see maestro?"
El Viejo alzó sus ojos al cielo, y los perdió:
"tonight I see too many things:
a society on the verge of total breakdown,
its psyche shredded by fictional anxieties . . ."
he continued with blank eyes:
"a clown cutting his fingers with scissors
a housewife emasculating her husband for the camera
a blond rastafarian setting himself on fire
a Republican político chasing Mexican boys
a performance artist named Guillermo devouring his
          own tongue . . ."
Gran Vato drank another Bohemia

he then began to stumble
"excerpts, missing excerpts . . .
the best parts of the film are missing tonight
& my tongue, my cobra tongue, is out of control . . .
(*alcoholic pause*)
yes, tonight I see too many things carnalito
& I'm having a hard time piecing them together."

XI: LA TELE PUES . . .

GP'S FACE ON MAIN VIDEO SCREEN. APOCALYPTIC SCENES
OF DEVASTATION ON OTHER SCREEN.

NEWSCASTER VOICE (WITH DELAY EFFECT):
good evening California
good morning Europe
we welcome the new century
with exciting family events:
tornados on the evening news
an earthquake, 6.7 this time
not the Big One yet
& to keep you awake tonight
we've got unprecedented inflation
robo-rangers riding missiles
narco-videots pendencieros
samurais, transformers y mojados
todos contra todos
within & vice versa
fire again
from TJ to Ventura
pólvora, hypnosis, doughnuts with arsénico
120 Mexicans on death row
channel 12, Televisión Amiga

serial murder enters La Placita
dressed as a pregnant nun
randomly killing 35 paisanos
an eight-year-old suburban wunderkind
murders his parents, neighbors, and toys
claims he ate too much ice cream
and receives 2,000 letters of support
a day in the life of Califas
we'll be back after you leave
with more asbestos, colera, teluride
HIV, nasal sex, pesticides
mexi-cide, other-cide,
the other side,
Riverside, Topanga, Malibu
Hollywood in shock
another day in the life of Califas
la mansión de la muerte
NBC reports . . .
(tongues/static)
the other is nowhere to be found
no towels or extra identities to spare
no place to hide & wait
no more placebos or instant utopias
Bali *(sighing)* became a tourist bordello
Oaxaca, a cheap clinic for lost franchutes
Taos & Tepoztlan, workshops for an imminent suicide
San Juan, the capital of high security
Havana, the mega-industry of marxist porn
your barrio, South Central, West Beirut
my gland, my liver . . .
it's all in my liver and my pen
even my pain

my finger whispers . . .
(whispering)
"still afraid of being alive, but I love it!"
"still afraid of YOU, S., lone-li-ness, but I love it!"
"still afraid of the way YOU look at me,
with a combination of anger & lust"
"still afraid to let you know how much I want . . .
to . . .
to be naked with Gloria Trevi
or Selena with a ski mask
for a month or so,
away from the daily wars
without even leaving the house for cappuccino
. . . the telephone unhooked; the computer unplugged
and a pile of CDs of Caetano, La Portuaria & Jello Biafra
to spice the cachondeo final
to fuck with insolencia
to truly embrace
the glo-ba-li-za-tion of crisis
amén
P.S. : we are still here
we will remain here until we die,
sin cartera,
sin temores, sin pasaporte . . .

XII: THE LAST TIME

MUSIC: DANZON IMPOSIBLE OR A MEXICAN WALTZ.

. . . & every night
for the next month
she woke up in my arms
La Chuca de la Condesa herself

"to remember in your arms
is an act of political defiance"
she whispered into my navel
"but this is the last time," I said
"nunca más habrémos de separarnos
I mean it"
but this time — I thought to myself —
the "it" was much harder to define
I wrote on my lap-top:

> *it, meaning migration . . . minus memory perhaps*
> *joy without ritual or purpose*
> *perpetual misunderstandings onstage*
> *it, meaning a dying era,*
> *a fading history,*
> *erratic economics,*
> *melancholic sex*
> *acid rain*
> *clumsy quebradita steps*
> *fraudulent elections,*
> *unexpected border check points*

(I pant & howl)
so, so, so, . . . "sexo!"
gritó el evangelista por la radio
EPIPHANIC VOICE/EVANGELIST PREACHER:

> *"amaos vivos y muertos*
> *cojaos los unos a los otros*
> *chupaos verguenzas y oquedades"*

so we kept making love like frightened coyotes
'til it was time (for one of us) to part once more
(de-part,
the largest col-lec-tive suicide)

rumbo a Phoenix, Chicago, Manhattan
y luego a Londres, Bilbao, Bruxelles,
Hamburgo & finally Berlin,
where the nights become magma
and the punks are simply gorgeous

MUSIC: GERMAN ROCK, SLOWLY BECOMING ROMANTIC
NORTEÑO MUSIC.

great tour;
lots of parties & reviews
its a pity
they hate me up here
'cause I look like a Turkish intellectual
dark, pensive, wounded, demanding . . .

BLACKOUT.

"dear audience:
in order to continue this performance,
I demand a translator, de ya!
is there anyone out there in performance limbo
who speaks German with a Mexican accent?"

XIII: LECCIÓN DE GEOGRAFÍA FINISECULAR

dear reader/dear audience
repeat with me out loud:
México es California
Marruecos es Madrid
Pakistan es Londres
Argelia es Paris
Cambodia es San Francisco
Turquia es Frankfurt
Puerto Rico es Nueva York

Centroamerica es Los Angeles
Honduras es New Orleans
Argentina es Paris
Beijing es San Francisco
Haiti es Nueva York
Nicaragua es Miami
Chiapas es Irlanda
your house is also mine
your language mine as well
& your heart will be mine
one of these nights
es la fuerza del sur
el Sur en el Norte
el Norte se desangra
el Norte se evapora
por los siglos de los siglos
& suddenly you're homeless
you've lost your land again
estimado antipaisano
your present dilemma is
to wander
in a transient geography de locos
without a flashlight
without a clue
sin visa, ni flota
joder

XIV: RADIO-POEMA

SATANIC VOICE:
infect, oh Mexicannis
infect those güeros tercos

against the will of history
inféctenlos tonight!
in fact, at this point in time
we have no other option but to be contagious
(con la lengua, el pito y la cultura)

my fearful radioescuchas,
apunten:
it's me again, el virus mostachón
el vato invader from the Martian South
La Momia Azteca reencarnada
& I'm everywhere partut
in your food, your dreams, your asshole
in the morning coffee & the evening news
for all the wrong reasons
I am here/there
to help you remember
the way this whole desmadre got started
in the first place

it's 1847,
& the world still spins in Spanish, carnal

XV: TAG

René wrote the best tag in the alley:
    one country, many nations
    many races, one big mess
— "a mystical one," I continued
in one of my many voices
a racist voice
a raunchy vocecita that goes like this:
(*singing in a parody of Japanese*)

& we kept singing karaoke at a transvestite bar
until the sun rose over the Mission
rima *(I hesitate & snap my fingers)*
& the Serbian snipers ran out of ammunition

XVI: A CLASSIFIED AD IN THE VOID

exit means salida
salida o triunfo
éxito or success
so exit the theater
or die triunfante
que la salida es al sur
y el éxito a la derecha, n'est-ce pas?
(I get unnecessarily romantic)
ay! exit-arte, exitarme sin éxito
gabacha de mis sueños profilactic
I write to you sabroso, tendido
I place a classified ad in the void:

>   *El Go-Mex/tizo boy, servidor de aquellas*
>   *con su lengua de obsidiana, bien filossa*
>   *busca güera bilingüe perdida en sí misma*
>   *he cries for you,*
>   *demands your tender understanding*
>   *so send a photo re-tocada*
>   *'cause he's very, very demanding*

the next day NAFTA came into effect
& I wrote on my lap-top:

>   *the only bridge left between Mexico & the U.S.*
>   *es el sexo, digo, el burrito afrodisiaco.*
>   *lo demás es academia. punto final*

XVII: OLD BORDER LETTER

looking for the primal source of my melancholy
I open a drawer
& find a letter dated September '80
a year & a half after my move to California
predating my Chicano identity
I quote:

> *querida M:*
> *(I wonder who is this M who appears in so many*
> *poems of mine)*
> *E.U. construye 7 bombas por hora*
> *inconcebibles en su refinamiento*
> *Nantli Ixtaccíhuatl aún no se embaraza*
> *y Quetzalcóatl el muy víbora*
> >   *no quiere regresar*
> *Madre Muerte Inmaculada*
> *que pianito electrocutas . . .*
> *los pendejos esperamos*
> *seguimos esperando y escribiendo*
> *waiting & writing*
> *aquí*
> *al noroeste de la página*
>
> *P.D. : la migra me trae finto*
> *mi identidad esta un poco inflamada*
> *y el café americano me sabe a orines*

XVIII: LOST ANGELES DIABÓLICOS

I'm back in L.A.
el lay que nunca vino
y nunca llegará

L.A./ "no lay," remember!
in mandarin, "mai-cuo" (misspelled),
"U.S." means "not a country,"
"L.A.," "not a city"
my house, "not even a house"
in other words
I'm not really back in Los Angeles
for this pinche city does not really exist.
STREET-WISE VOICE:
it's all a project bro, a corporate bucolia
to put it bluntly
a convoluted plot concocted by criminals, lawyers,
policemen, políticos, phony actors with toupees
they see no difference between sports & war
& join cults to make life bearable
you've seen them on TV
all-American boys with big weapons & small aspirations
afraid of losing control
of losing themselves in another culture,
another airport,
another lover,
another trip to Río or Yucatán

interface:
the drunk tourist approaches a sexy señorrita at "El
        Faisan" club:
GRINGOÑOL:
"oie prreciosa, my Mayan queen
tu estarr muchio muy bela
con tu ancient fire en la piel
parra que io queme mis bony fingers
mi pájarra belísima

216

io comprou tu amor con mía mastercard"
she answers in impeccable French:
"ne me derange plus ou jai vous arrache les yeux!"

XIX: THE SOURCE OF THEIR HATRED

they hate me for writing like this
they hate me for knowing exactly who I am
for being so openly fragile & direct
for putting my dirty finger in their ancient wounds
for not ever wanting to go back
or not knowing exactly where to go back
& when I write in tongues
they hate me even more
(tongues)
I write like this
porque mi lengua esta partida
(tongues)
ésta partida . . .
my very last departure
partiture du merde
hacia el otro lado de la niebla
1955–1995
un míto mas
un mexicano menos
frito, finito . . .
SOS,
es puro pedo

"Greetings from La Chola Coqueta y La Charromántica" (Roberto Sifuentes and Gómez-Peña) Washington, D.C., 1995. Photo by Charles Steck

XX: PERFORMANCE

Day of the Dead/downtown San Diego
I take off my silk shirt
written in blood on my chest dice:
    there used to be a Mexican inside this body
an INS body bag lies next to my snakeskin boots
stenciled with black letters remata:
    Courtesy of Governor Wilson
next morning, the photo caption reads:
    performance art overlaps with raw politics
a wooden Indian observes the scene quietly

scene #2010:
"he was a bad poet"
— a critic whispered at the funeral —
"a minority impersonator
a Benetton primitive
a ready-made Indian
GRINGOÑOL:
cuassi brujou de la palabra you know
he came to America to get laid
to take advantage of our innocence
but now he plays mariachi muzak in Hell"

XXI: "LA FLOATING FLOTA VS. EL CIRCULO DE THOR"
OR "LA SINRAZON DE VIVIR AL BORDE DE OCCIDENTE"

early evening, Long Beach, 40 centigrades
a homeless man from Laos pisses on a rotten shrimp
the Spur Possy surrounds him
beats him to death as if he were a conga
then sets him on fire as if he were a pagan god

WAR DRUMS IN CRESCENDO.

a black man passes by on skates whistling "La Marsellaise"
"typical, typical Los Angeles," he says
violencia sin antecedentes
imágen pura sin contenido
"ironía," comments my carnalito, Rubén
"100 percent ironía."
(*pause*)
"the homeless are howling in the distance
can you hear them?" I ask my audience
"they wish they were here tonight
tonight is the last night on earth
for many, many people"
(*unbearable pause*)
my audience is deeply hurt
ni pedo.

XXII: MISSING EXCERPTS

. . . excerpts, missing excerpts
the best parts of the film are missing again
& my tongue, my cobra tongue, is out of control:
"I fuck
you fuck
they fuck
we all fuck each other
they all fuck each other over
we all slowly die
we all slowly bury one another"
no, we will never make it back to the old house. period.
it's labor day in Rwanda
a day without art in America

& the Mexican army approaches Guadalupe-Tepeyac

SCENES OF MILITARY PARACHUTERS DESCENDING ON THE
CHIAPANECA JUNGLE ON THE VIDEO SCREEN, ACCOMPANIED
BY BASQUE ROCK 'N' ROLL.

XXIII: PIRATE MESSAGES ON THE SHORT-WAVE RADIO

MUFFLED VOICES WITH STATIC.

ciudadanos de la amnesia
hemos perdido la paciencia histórica
estar y esperar no es suficiente
cambio.
GRINGOÑOL:
we are about to take over the streets
about to take over the station
cambio.
RADIO ANNOUNCER:
Tequila Cuervo Añejo
for the contemporary warrior
who doesn't want to give up
his language, his clarity, his costume
cambio.
we all are involved in a hunger strike
'cause we need to lose some weight ipso facto
cambio.
tired of suffering from political outrage
& not having a language to express it?
call Dr. Nancy Dharma
she'll help you find your inner activist
cambio.
vato

when are you going to defect?
many embassies are dying to take you
imagine a Mexican in Taiwan or Botswana
cambio. fuera

XXIV: PHONE CALL

SOFT VOICE:
"It's me loca
burning with doubts
don't ask me where I am or
why I'm asking you these questions
just tell me yes or no, te lo suplico:
will you still love me if I go to jail?
will you dare to love a pinto existencial?
what if I get shot by a cop
who happens to mistake me for Guillermo, el otro,
el que nunca partió
& end up a five-second red note in the evening news?
I mean it's cold and dangerous up north . . .
(interference)
will you remember me after my imminent departure?"
(more interference)
partir, depart, de-por-ta-ción?
"alo? hellooo? operator?
I was talking to my . . .
but . . . the line got . . .
mixed up with other po . . . poems . . .
fuck it! you're losing me or vice versa
I just can't hear you any more!
loocccaaaa!!!!"

XXV: MEMORY

Madrid, Café Jijón, 9:00 A.M.
I sip my coffee, catatonic
to the music of Toreros Muertos
while writing on a napkin:
> *the missiles are pointing at Baghdad*
> *bombs dancerly falling over Somalia*
> *NAFTA businessmen stampede into Mexico*
> *L.A. cops perform their sexy roles for the camera*
> *& suddenly, a gun, a silver Magnum*
> *pointing at your forehead*
I address my other self rhetorically:
> *". . . and you can't even see*
> *whose finger's on the trigger carnal?"*

(close-up) my tongue is black again
a scary-looking tourist sits at my table
& out of the blue he says,
"you know, we're living a permanent crisis"
"I know, but your crisis is worse than mine"
I answer
I, I, I dare to finish the pinche paragraph
my, my, my leather vest is covered with blood
chi-chi-chicken blood to be precise
me, me, dicen el Gallo Pendenciero
el Vatorcido dans la rue de la chingada
I, I, I win every battle on stage
s-s-small battles, mi-minute ones,
but they somehow count . . .
pause
my audience waits for some real action

(next morning smells like sulfur & tar
the headlines read: "The ETA leadership prefers Coke")

XXVI: INTERROGATION

NASAL VOICE/OPEN ARMS:
three fat cops during the heat wave
pull out their iron dildos
the interrogation begins
cameras one & two, rolling . . .
down my psyche . . .
SLOW VOICE, EXHAUSTED/SCREAMS OF PAIN
      IN THE BACKGROUND:
my new code # is 000-842517
why?!
the social security fucked up
the telephone company fucked up as well
& so did the INS, the IRS, the NSA,
the DEA, the NRA, SOS . . .
& so did MGM, the PRI and MOMA
they all fucked up real bad
& now we're left with a bunch of
untranslatable acronyms
to fill the empty space ahead
to provide la vida loca ahead
with some decent format & direction
"¿a que vida te refieres?" — me preguntan
la vida sin tregua ni contenido
la vida en el epicentro de la herida
la vida, bien Ammerrican, you know
la vida, real nasty aquí en el corazón
"can you be more specific?"

life, out of a suitcase again
life on a bare stage
life between songs & projects
entre kisses & stabbings
entre azúl y buenas noches
arrivals & departures
sperm & Scotch
la vida sin-taxis chola
la vida sin visa improvisando
in the hardest of times
of the hardest year
of the strangest decade of EFA
"cut! cut!
what do you mean by EFA?"
— the hooded man asks me
you know, sultán,
Estados Flotantes de Aztlán
a new name for a new country
EFFFFFFFFFFFFFAAAA
cambio de canal:
my fragile home
collapses over my other selves
it's a 7.5 quake this time
& the stage is filled with rubble
I walk in total darkness
on my Catholic knees
& cry for a vision

XXVII: THE VISION

a dark man bigotón in a zebra-skin tuxedo
w/ a boa around his neck bien sleazoide

walks in slow motion across the flaming stage
goes by the name of "Quebradito,"
confesses to his audience parsimonioso:
"they gave us drugs & guns
they hired us to do menial jobs
like cleaning, singing, cooking & gardening
the salaries were crappy
they collected half of them in taxes
forced us to buy insurance for this & that
& then they called the migra on us
& when we fought back
they said we were violent & ungrateful"
— he looks intensely at an audience member
"you call this democracia mister?"
the audience member shoots him in the forehead
blackout!
he wasn't a plant
believe me, he wasn't a plant
performance is merely another way to tell the truth
often to the detriment of poetry

XXVIII: CRUCIAL MEMORY

"get a ticket back to Mexico,
& if you can't
get a poster of democracy at least

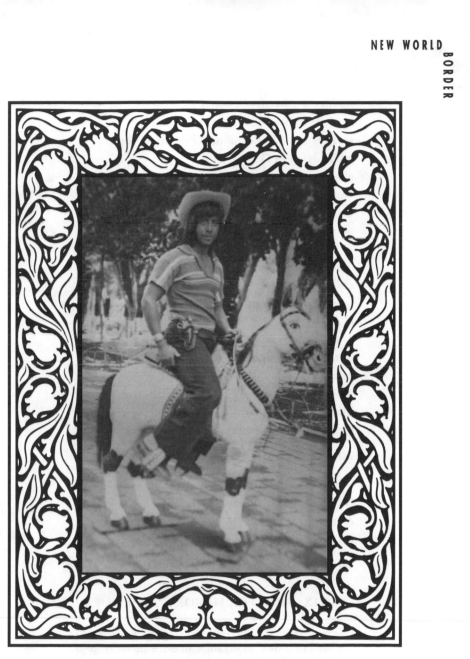

First self-conscious performative gesture. Gómez-Peña as "El Vaquero Poblano," Puebla, 1975.

but dream, dream of a better place
no dejes nunca de soñar . . . en español"
said my uncle Carlos, automobile union leader
while dying in Detroit
alone among bigots and broken records
"mujer, tell the neighbors
we were never that evil . . . or dirty"
— he told my aunt Roberta while he was dying in
      Detroit —
"show them the poems of my nephew
el Charromántico
que aulla en el escenario"
(*I howl*)
& she did
but my poems didn't sit very well
in the stomach of those bigots.
punto.
like a million others
Carlos died three months away from Mexico

DIM LIGHTS/A SAD BOLERO.

sometimes a Mexican funeral
is just an illegible postcard
& it tends to arrive
three months after the fact

TOTAL DARKNESS/TOTAL SILENCE. NOTHING TO ADD.

XXIX: VIDEO OR MEMORY, ¿QUÉ PUES?

carnal, facts are unbearable these days. like ants, they
are hard to codify, to organize in one's memory, &
the lap-top doesn't really help. random facts are what

we have to contend with. impossible for the time being
to extract poetry from them.
therefore I turn on the video monitor
I mean my memory
I mean the video
I mean

BLURRY IMAGE APPEARS ON VIDEO SCREEN.

Palenque, Summer of 1975
I thought I was in love when I first arrived in the jungle
a child of the Mexican crisis
in search of the tropical *welchtmertz*
(but not the German one).
I rented a cottage made out of straw
I observed my penis swell day after day
. . . the effect of the heat & the mosquitoes
(one single mosquito
could make you hallucinate for hours)
I walked every day without purpose or shirt
I was looking for X'tabay, her bittersweet fruits
I was also looking for my three other lost selves
but instead I found an installation of Petroleos
& a bunch of burnouts from Europe & New York
who thought I had precisely what they were looking for

(2 pages of illegible text)

. . . thus the road was my salvation
& performance meant the possibility of connecting
all these places and facts in a somewhat coherent manner
meeting people with slightly similar concerns:
performance, language, activismo, geografía,
spiders, phony tribal artifacts, aficionado archeology & shit

therefore I parted again
this time to the sierra Tarahumara
Raramuri, Mater Dei Dolorosa
amén
twenty years later . . .
still writing, de milagro
in a Boulder coffee shop:

> *my skeleton screams inside of me*
> *SCRATCHY VOICE:*
> *"ay, where to go back sultán?*
> *Manhattan, San Pancho, Tijuana,*
> *Mexico City or even before . . .*
> *Tehuixtla, Palenque, Oaxaca . . .*
> *empty words in foreign ears*
> *blurry pintas sprayed on our psyches*
> *where & how to end this journey carnal?"*

> *my skeleton is out of his fucking mind*
> *talks to me as if I was someone else*

XXX: EL HAMLET FRONTERIZO

TWO VOICES:
me ama/ no me ama
me caso/no me caso
me canso/ no me canso
chicano o mexicano
que soy o me imagino
regreso o continúo
me mato/ no me mato
en Mexico/ en Califas
to write or to perform

in English or in Spanish . . .
I forgive you,
I crave you
ansiosamente tuyo,
de nadie mas
frontera mediante . . .
te espero, mi loca, te sigo esperando . . .
you are it, tu sangre, tus cicatrices . . .

XXXI: MALDICIÓN

September 16, 1990, San Anto, outdoor conjunto fest.
I see myself in the features of a child
his future self preceding my broken selves
people wear every costume I ever wore
a pre-recorded voice I never heard before
comes out of the loud speaker
FILTERED VOICE:
"your future will collapse
in a drive-by shooting
or an anal kiss,
like this (*I snap my fingers*)
& the great Aztec divinities will have to judge you
on the basis of your sexual, social, & aesthetic behavior
punto. let's see you get out of that one"
nota de consolación I write on my left arm:
    most crimes are misguided gestures of resistance

whose future is HE talking about? — I ask one of
        my other selves
& whose voice is it?
not mine
my real voice is . . .

231

not mine either
I mean,
I'm just an oracle, raza
me dicen "El Pitonizo"
por lo de aquello, tu sabes
& tonight the Great Netzahualcóyotl speaks through
     my gañote
ajjuua!
téhuatl titla huancapol

XXXII: IT'S ALL IN HIGH-8, FRÄULEIN

the evangelist was sobbing at the plaza
he witnessed an apparition
an unfamiliar world of lies unfolding in front of him
& somewhere in the middle of the vision
a blinking Virgen Chola in garter belt la primorosa
he couldn't take it any more
he heard Gregorian chants emerging from the ground
scratched & mixed with the voices of his criminal ancestors
then he peed in his pants, el Jim whatever, tejano del Infierno.

I thought of the Popol Vuh, the German band, not the book
I thought of Mishima for some stupid reason
I thought of "Jesus and Mary Chain"
I remembered Den Passar
Vladivostok, Tapachula
San Luis Colorado,
San Sebastian
lusting for Marina Abramovich
slam-dancing flamenco in Hamburg
eating enchiladas on tinfoil
at a truck stop in Iowa

Amanas, I believe,
another failed utopia
a bad cartoon of Germany
50 centrigrades of angst
stop!
the North evaporates
aaayyy!!
cum¡¡¡
tengo una polución
(*mistranslation*)
the word is so polluted
the U.S., beyond reconstruction
the elders wait around the fire

INDIAN CHANTS IN A DYING LANGUAGE.

clearly they will outlive us all
Pirimicua, Pachamama, Eleguá
Quetzalcóatl, Changó, Banto-cheya
when will you vatos down there
come back to feed us?
we are starving for clarity.
(Herzog never shot that scene
but I recorded it in high-8
during one of my many trips
to the end of Western Civilization)

XXXIII: LOVE POEM

jaina. the last time I opened your legs
I saw the end of the world for a second

XXXIV: LOSING IT ON STAGE

. . . I suddenly forget the script.
(I begin to improvise)
de-de-dear audience:
do you know where are we meant to go tonight?
(long pause; I scream for the house lights)
is there a hot concierto
somewhere in this unbearable city?
(no one answers)
where will I be at the end of this text?
(two people stand up and leave)
will I be deaf, mad, or somewhat incomplete?
(five more people leave)
will my oldest house still be standing?
will my adored mother ever return from Thailand?
(people continue to walk out)
will my friends be dying of AIDS or random bullets?
on whose breasts will I be resting next century?
on whose land will I be resting for good?
is it true that the very day I finish this text
my heart will suddenly cease to pound?
(total silence)
answer me!
fuckin' answer me!!
*(the theater is empty by now; I am screaming at the top of
     my lungs)*
I'm a religious creature after all
I demand theological answers de ya!
*(I adopt a fetal position on the ground & begin to sob like
     a baby)*
pronto

cambio di locazione:
I wake up in a pink Holiday Inn hotel room
who knows where chingados
the telephone is ringing
"Mr. Gómez, the people next door have complained
that you or someone else in your room or inside of you
is screaming obscenities in a foreign language . . ."

I hang up. I'm out of ink & cigarettes . . .

XXXV: PERFORMANCE

JACKALOPE MUSIC.

Scottsdale, Arizona, early '94
I pray to a dead chicken
"chick, chick, chick-en oh
Chi-cano Pater Deus del Terror
provide us with the necessary chiles to continue
enough stubborness to survive
& lots of verbo to put up a good fight"
third call. the performance begins . . .
y la zozobra

I sit inside a plexiglass box
surrounded by crickets & snakes
a bunch of cowboys, Mormons & others look at me
some kneel & confess their fears into the mike
an elegant lady confesses her lust for my ancient legs
I whisper a fragment of an old poem:
> *"hoy no cruzaremos la frontera*
> *hoy no saldremos en busca de lo insólito*
> *hoy habremos de permanecer inmóviles*
> *en este mausoleo facticio*

> — *la identidad así congelada* —
> *hasta que la Muerte nos visite"*

THE LIGHTS GO OUT.

(my audience experiences panic. . . .)

TO BE CONTINUED IN MY NEXT BOOK . . .

TO BE FINISHED THE DAY I DIE . . .

Performance remains. Highways, 1993. Photo by Elia Arce

WHERE WERE YOU DURING ALL THOSE YEARS?

yes, Matachin, I was there when I was born
I happened to be there at the right time
I stepped out of my mother's depths
& ipso facto I began to complain
it was the year that the Angel of Independence fell
        down . . .
(you may remember that journalists were astonished
        by the fact that he didn't bleed at all)
I was also there when a hurricane
with a gorgeous female name hit Isla Mujeres
& the roof of my cabin flew away like in a Chinese
        dream . . .

I was there during the 2nd Mexico City earthquake
carrying coffins from the police station to the
        morgue & back
no big deal Califa
I had already been to America
thus I knew about silence & death . . .

indeed I was there when Manhattan went bankrupt . . .
when the skinheads were burning Turks in Germany
gypsies in Spain, and rockeros in Buenos Aires . . .
(me salvé de milagro)

238

yes, I went to bed with so & so
but at the time I had no other options . . .
(era como jugar a la ruleta rusa)

I missed the L.A. riots by a week
(I was on display as an "authentic Amerindian" in
     Madrid)
but I was there
when the last American dream crumbled in Los
     Angeles
it was Martin Luther King Day
a 6.7 earthquake
and half of my memories were shattered in a few
     seconds
including this text & other much better ones
that I was unable to rewrite
but I was there & that's what counts, ¿que no? . . .

of course I was there when my father was buried in '89
I had to be there with my just-born child for
     continuity's sake
I was a child myself of the great American crises . . .
at the time my job description stated:
"fearless . . . exuberant . . . melancholic . . . intertextual
meant to document the birth pains of the new milennium
the death of rock 'n' roll, & the completion of all Indian
*   prophecies*
meant to allow other voices to emerge out of his open
*   stomach*
to howl on stage & to get paid for doing so"

Matachin, I did my best, I did my very best . . .
by the way, where were you during all those years?

GLOSSARY OF BORDERISMOS

alien A term used by opportunistic politicians and sleazy reporters to describe any legal or illegal immigrant, people with heavy accents or exotic clothes, and people who exhibit eccentric social, sexual, or aesthetic behavior.

amigoization Process of happy Mexicanization currently taking place in the U.S. Southwest. This phenomenon was first detected by Gran Vato José Antonio Burciaga, Minister of Information of the seceding Republik of Berkeley. The opposite of "borderization."

Art-mageddon The end of the world according to the art world, or the end of the art world itself.

Aztec High-Tech, El Undercover antropoloco, apocalyptic disc-jockey and cross-cultural salesman. Poses as a performance artist. Goes by the dubious names of "The Warrior for Gringostroika," "El Naftazteca" and "El Quebradito." Gringos often call him Gwermo Go-Mex Piña or Yiguermo Comes Penis. His mother calls him Bill.

Aztlán The "original land" in Aztec mythology. According to Chicano poets it was located in what now is the U.S. Southwest. Also, the name of a trucking company in East L.A.

borderígena A citizen of the great border region of the Americas, o sea, you & I and all the pinche raza we know.

borderization Self-explanatory. Currently afflicting the U.S. and Western Europe, this process is also known by sociologists as "Calcuttization" or "tercermundización."

border pop A transnational music and fashion movement that encompasses, among other loqueras and rhythms, punkarachi,

240

heavy nopal, rapguango, mambop, jarochabilly, techno-banda, huapunkgo and the bizarre Tex-Mex Banghra movement.

Canochi An upside-down or inverted Chicano, meaning, a Mexican who has become Chicanized (or Chicano-ized?) without ever having to leave Mexico.

Chica-lango Half Chicano and half "chilango" (a derogative term for a hegemonic Mexico City hipster who happens to believe that Mexico City is the center of the continent — even if it is true).

Chicanadians Second generation Mexicans living in Canada and/or children of Mexican and Canadian parents living in the U.S. Please do not confuse this term with "Can-aliens," which refers to any undocumented Canadian, inside or outside of Canada.

culti-multuralism An esperantic Disneyworldview in which all cultures, races and sexes live happily together. Coined by Chicano antropoloco Robert Sánchez, the term went out of use in 1992.

Cybervato, El Seditious accomplice of "El Naftazteca," media pirate and information super-highway bandido. Goes by the name of Bob Sifuentes.

desmodernidad From the Spanish noun *desmadre* (meaning being motherless, or living in permanent chaos). Coined by post-Mexican antropoloco Roger Bartra.

Empty-V After Reali-TV, the second largest media conglomerate on the planet.

Free Raid Agreement Whoops! Just a typo, ese.

Free Taco Agreement An innovative economic initiative designed by The Chicano Secret Service. Its main objective is the production and distribution of free tacos to the starving and deterritorialized gringo minorities. En español, "Tratado de Libre Comerse." Favor de no confundirlo con el (intraducible) "Tratando de Libre Cogerse."

Funkahuatl The Aztec god of funk and night life. Alter-ego of East Los Chicano rocker Rubén Guevara.

ganga From the English word "gang," a term used by police departments in the U.S. to describe all people of color under 18.

gringolatra S/he who adores gringos.

gringostroika A continental grassroots movement that advocates the complete economic and cultural reform of U.S. anarcho-capitalism.

Gringotlani(teca) Nomadic Anglo tribesmen who migrated to southern Mexico and Guatemala in the early '70s. They are known for their colorful ponchos, stylish huaraches, and encyclopedic knowledge of Latino culture in general.

hanging chickens, los In the 19th century, the sinister Texas Rangers and a white supremacist vigilante organization called the White Caps used to lynch Mexican migrant workers, who were then referred to as *"pollos."* The term is still used throughout the southwestern United States. Any other political, metaphysical, erotic or artistic interpretations of the chickens hanging onstage during Gómez-Peña's performances are welcomed by the author.

horror vacui Please ask Umberto Eco or Jean Baudrillard.

jaina Spanglishization of "honey." Sweetheart, novia, torta, chava, chuca, mi locota, etc.

jalapeño pusher A petty criminal who sells chiles on the streets to intoxicate innocent American children.

kilombo Independent micro-republics created by runaway slaves in the 17th and 18th centuries. Kilombos which have survived into the present include East L.A., Pilsen (Chicago), Little Oaxaca, and the Bronx.

Krishnahuatl The Aztec god of karma, in exile in the Bay Area.

Latinos Alpinos Latino settlements in the Swiss Alps and the Rocky Mountains. Also, the name of a Chilean postpunk band.

maquiladora art A model of production often used by cultural organizations based on the United States side of the border: Mexican and Chicano artists provide raw talent, while gringos administer the operation.

ménage à trade Synonymous with NAFTA.

Mexkimo A polar Mexican. Mexkimo settlements are found in what used to be Iowa, Minnesota, Illinois, and British Columbia. First identified by Chicago poet Carlos Cumpian.

Miki Mikiztli Califas Náhuatl for "California, the house of death."

NAFTArt A cultural initiative of all three NAFTA countries in which art is utilized as a form of conservative diplomacy, and also to create conflict-free national images in order to seduce foreign investors and cultural tourists.

othercide The murder of otherness.

pene-trading The act of trading with a smaller and weaker country. It also refers to the act of trading male genitalia.

performear Spanglish for "to piss on your audience."

performantli An Aztec tradition of involuntary performance art discovered by artist Maris Bustamante. Famous performantlecas include Los Xochimilcas, El Sup (Subcomandante Marcos) & the EZLN, Tin-Tán, Irma Serrano, Gloria Trevi, Selena, Ima Sumac, Superbarrio, and Fray Tormenta. (Dear reader, if you don't recognize any of these names, you are an incurable ethnocentrist.)

pocho S/he who bastardizes the Spanish language and Mexican aesthetics. Infamous pochos include the members of Culture Clash, The Chicano Secret Service, René Yañez, Sandra

Cisneros, Ana Castillo, Rubén Martínez, Nao Bustamante, and Guillermo Gómez-Peña.

post-CNN Chicano art A new techno-rascuache aesthetic that fuses epic rap poetry, performance art, interactive television, holographic radio, and computer art, but with a chicanocentric perspective and a sleazoid bent.

pus-modernity The infected modernity, according to chilango antropolocos Rogelio Villareal and Mongo.

Saint Frida (Kahlo) Holy Patroness of ethno-feminists and NAFTArt dealers.

sexual democracia A Latin American version of democracy in which political decisions are made according to sexual desire.

Spanglishization A continental infection for which there is no cure.

Supermojado Border hero, conceptual carnal of Superbarrio, champion of undocumented workers' rights, and archenemy of Migrasferatu and Pito Wilson.

television White people's freedom of speech.

Vatoman Chicano Batman. Colleague of Supermojado and lover of La Batichica de Mexicali.

virtual barrio The Chicano Inter-neta.

white list A secret list that includes members of the opposition to the New World Border, as well as militant monoculturalists.

END-OF-THE-CENTURY TOPOGRAPHY REVIEW

FIRST WORLD

a tiny and ever shrinking conceptual archipelago from which 80% of the resources of our planet are still administered and controlled

SECOND WORLD

aka, "geo-political limbo," includes Greenland, the Antarctic continent, the oceans, the mineral world, and the dismembered Soviet Bloc

THIRD WORLD

the ex-underdeveloped countries, and the communities of color within the ex-First World

FOURTH WORLD

a conceptual place where the indigenous inhabitants of the Americas meet with the deterritorialized peoples, the immigrants, and the exiles; it occupies portions of all the previous worlds

FIFTH WORLD

virtual space, mass media, the U.S. suburbs, art schools, malls, Disneyland, the White House & La Chingada

(over)

QUESTIONS FOR THE READER:

Where exactly is the U.S. located?

In which world (or worlds) are YOU located?

Has your community been left out of the above categories?

For which world does your art speak?

Are you experiencing an identity crisis?

Please mail your answers to your local gringostroika representative or to City Lights Books.

Guillermo Gómez-Peña is an internationally acclaimed multimedia performance artist, social and cultural critic, and author. Born in 1955 and raised in Mexico City, he first came to the United States in 1978. Since then he has been exploring cross-cultural issues in his performance art, multilingual poetry, journalism, video, radio, and installation art.

Gómez-Peña was a founding member of the Border Arts Workshop/Taller de Arte Fronterizo (1985-1990), a contributor to the national radio program "Crossroads" (1987-1990), and editor of the experimental arts magazine *The Broken Line/La Linea Quebrada* (1985-1990). He is a regular contributor to the national radio news magazine "Latino U.S.A.," and contributing editor at *High Performance Magazine* and *The Drama Review*. He has received the Prix de la Parole, New York's Bessie Award, and the MacArthur Genius Award, among numerous other fellowships and prizes.

Gómez-Peña's performance work and critical writings have been instrumental in the development of the debates on cultural diversity, identity, and U.S.-Mexico relations. He has won a well-deserved reputation as one of the most effective interpreters of cultural otherness in the United States.

Other works by Gómez-Peña:

An earlier collection of performance texts, essays, and poems titled **Warrior for Gringostroika** was published in 1993 by Graywolf Press (Saint Paul, MN).

Performance work available on video: **Border Brujo, The Son of Border Crises,** and **Naftaztec TV** can be ordered from Video Data Bank (Chicago) 312-345-3550, or from V-Tape (Toronto, Ontario) 416-351-1317.

A double-CD collection of radio and audio work, **Borderless Radio** is available from Word of Mouth (Toronto, Ontario) 416-531-5070.

A multimedia catalog, **The Temple of Confessions: Mexican Beasts and Living Santos,** will be published by Powerhouse Books (New York) in October, 1996.

"This peripatetic "post-Mexican romantic" travels around the U.S. and the world practicing a performance art and preaching an intercultural gospel that brings the American melting pot to a boil"

— *American Theater Magazine*

Gómez-Peña's commitment to force North America to adjust to the South, to acknowledge the hemisphere's cultural imbalance, places him among the most significant of late-20th-century performance artists."

— *Voice Literary Supplement*

"Few performance artists deliver their opinions with as much punch and with such delightful verbal acrobatics."

— *San Antonio Light*

"He's a citizen of everywhere and nowhere, a post-Mexican, neo-Chicano, trans-American. These transitional identities feed the work, become the work.

—*Cindi Carr*

" His focus on U.S./Mexico relations has helped to inject the word "border" into the national arts discourse."

— *New York Times*

"His inventive efforts to create a hybrid culture have won him international acclaim." — *U.S. News & World Report*

CITY LIGHTS PUBLICATIONS

Mrabet, Mohammed. M'HASHISH
Murguía, A. & B. Paschke, eds. VOLCAN: Poems from Central America
Murillo, Rosario. ANGEL IN THE DELUGE
Nadir, Shams. THE ASTROLABE OF THE SEA
Parenti, Michael. AGAINST EMPIRE
Parenti, Michael. DIRTY TRUTHS
Pasolini, Pier Paolo. ROMAN POEMS
Pessoa, Fernando. ALWAYS ASTONISHED
Peters, Nancy J., ed. WAR AFTER WAR (City Lights Review #5)
Poe, Edgar Allan. THE UNKNOWN POE
Porta, Antonio. KISSES FROM ANOTHER DREAM
Prévert, Jacques. PAROLES
Purdy, James. THE CANDLES OF YOUR EYES
Purdy, James. GARMENTS THE LIVING WEAR
Purdy, James. IN A SHALLOW GRAVE
Purdy, James. OUT WITH THE STARS
Rachlin, Nahid. THE HEART'S DESIRE
Rachlin, Nahid. MARRIED TO A STRANGER
Rachlin, Nahid. VEILS: SHORT STORIES
Reed, Jeremy. DELIRIUM: An Interpretation of Arthur Rimbaud
Reed, Jeremy. RED-HAIRED ANDROID
Rey Rosa, Rodrigo. THE BEGGAR'S KNIFE
Rey Rosa, Rodrigo. DUST ON HER TONGUE
Rigaud, Milo. SECRETS OF VOODOO
Ross, Dorien. RETURNING TO A
Ruy Sánchez, Alberto. MOGADOR
Saadawi, Nawal El. MEMOIRS OF A WOMAN DOCTOR
Sawyer-Lauçanno, Christopher, transl. THE DESTRUCTION OF THE JAGUAR
Scholder, Amy, ed. CRITICAL CONDITION: Women on the Edge of Violence
Sclauzero, Mariarosa. MARLENE
Serge, Victor. RESISTANCE
Shepard, Sam. MOTEL CHRONICLES
Shepard, Sam. FOOL FOR LOVE & THE SAD LAMENT OF PECOS BILL
Smith, Michael. IT A COME
Snyder, Gary. THE OLD WAYS
Solnit, Rebecca. SECRET EXHIBITION: Six California Artists
Sussler, Betsy, ed. BOMB: INTERVIEWS
Takahashi, Mutsuo. SLEEPING SINNING FALLING
Turyn, Anne, ed. TOP TOP STORIES
Tutuola, Amos. FEATHER WOMAN OF THE JUNGLE
Tutuola, Amos. SIMBI & THE SATYR OF THE DARK JUNGLE
Valaoritis, Nanos. MY AFTERLIFE GUARANTEED
Veltri, George. NICE BOY
Waldman, Anne. FAST SPEAKING WOMAN
Wilson, Colin. POETRY AND MYSTICISM
Wilson, Peter Lamborn. SACRED DRIFT
Wynne, John. THE OTHER WORLD
Zamora, Daisy. RIVERBED OF MEMORY